# The Narrow Ground

# A. T. Q. STEWART

# The Narrow Ground

## ASPECTS OF ULSTER
## 1609–1969

FABER & FABER
3 Queen Square London

*First published in 1977*
*by Faber and Faber Limited*
*3 Queen Square London WC1*
*Printed in Great Britain by*
*Butler & Tanner Ltd*
*Frome and London*
*All rights reserved*

British Library Cataloguing in Publication Data

Stewart, Anthony Terence Quincey
    The narrow ground.
    1. Northern Ireland—History
    I. Title
    941.6          DA999.U46

ISBN 0-571-10325-1

To J. C. B.

# Contents

# Maps

# Author's Note

The purpose of this essay is to examine five aspects of Ulster history since 1609. It is not intended to be a comprehensive survey of the Ulster question, still less a history of Northern Ireland. The treatment is thematic rather than chronological, but each theme is centred on a significant historical episode, and the episodes are in chronological sequence—the Plantation of Ulster, the siege of Londonderry, the United Irish movement, Belfast riots in the nineteenth century, and partition. I have assumed that the reader already knows the outlines of Irish history and something of events in Northern Ireland since 1969. He is left to decide for himself what bearing, if any, the subjects discussed have had on the present troubles.

The extract from a document in *Aspects of Irish Social History, 1750–1800* on pp. 132–34 appears by permission of the Deputy Keeper of Records for Northern Ireland, Mr. B. I. Trainor and the co-editor, Mr. W. H. Crawford.

*I never saw a richer country, or, to speak my mind, a finer people; the worst of them is the bitter and envenomed dislike which they have to each other. Their factions have been so long envenomed, and they have such narrow ground to do their battle in, that they are like people fighting with daggers in a hogshead.*

SIR WALTER SCOTT, 1825

# Retrospect

On the morning of 7 December 1688 an advance party of the Earl of Antrim's regiment reached the waterside on the right bank of the Foyle opposite Derry. Two of the officers, a lieutenant and an ensign, crossed the river by the ferry and, presenting warrants directed to the mayor and sheriffs, demanded admittance and quarters for His Majesty's soldiers. For several weeks now the city of Londonderry had been without a garrison, since the withdrawal of Lord Mountjoy's Regiment of Foot. Mountjoy's men had been for the most part Protestants, and in 1688 the Lord Deputy of Ireland, the Earl of Tyrconnell, was engaged in removing all the Protestant officers from the Irish army and replacing them with Catholics. On the instructions of King James II he had also raised a new regiment in each of the four Irish provinces. The regiment in Ulster was commanded by Alexander MacDonnell, the Catholic Earl of Antrim, and was recruited from his Irish followers and Scottish highlanders, all of them Catholic.

The news in the first days of December that this force of 1,200 men, with a large number of women and children, was moving towards Derry to secure the city's allegiance to the King in the coming struggle with William, the Prince of Orange, caused great concern among the Protestants within the walled city. For days, rumours had been circulating. It was said that the Irish in the neighbourhood had been collecting pikes and knives; friars had been preaching sermons alluding to the slaughter of the Amalekites. Anxiety was not allayed when it became known that an anonymous letter found far away in the streets of Comber, Co. Down, and addressed to a Protestant nobleman, had warned that on 9 December the Irish would fall upon Protestants and planters, and kill them man, wife and child. These hastily raised soldiers of Lord Antrim were kin to the men who had attacked the Protestant settlers in the Rebellion of 1641.

Thus when it was seen that the officers' warrants were not

signed, the anxious sheriffs seized on the pretext to play for time. An excited debate was taking place among crowds gathered in the market square. Many of the younger citizens were for keeping the regiment out, and even some of the aldermen, though fearful of the consequences, hoped that this might be done without their having to take the lead. The waiting soldiers on the opposite bank, suspecting some such design, now began to cross the river in considerable numbers and move swiftly towards the city walls. Suddenly, when the first of them were within sixty yards of the Ferry Gate, a group of thirteen apprentices ran to the main guard, seized the keys, and drawing up the bridge, shut and locked the gate. Then they hastened to shut the other three great gates of the city, leaving an armed guard on each. Though the city was not closely invested until the following April, this exclusion of King James's soldiers marked the beginning of the famous siege of Londonderry, which was not raised until August 1689.

On 12 August 1969 the Apprentice Boys of Derry celebrated the lifting of the siege by their annual parade on the city walls. The political atmosphere in Northern Ireland was extremely bad, worse than it had been since 1922, as a consequence of the accelerating Catholic civil rights agitation which had led to clashes with the police in 1968. The Apprentice Boys and the Orange Order had turned down requests from the government to cancel their processions. It was widely forecast that if they took place, there would be serious disorders, and even an uprising of the entire Catholic population. This prophecy proved to be true. As the Orangemen marched through the centre of the walled city, stones began to rain down upon their heads, thrown by crowds of Catholic rioters who had assembled for the purpose. The parade broke up in disorder, and serious rioting developed. When the police, issued with steel helmets and riot shields, tried to drive the mobs back into the Catholic districts beyond the walls, they were repulsed again and again with stones and petrol-bombs.

After forty-eight hours a scene appeared in Derry which no one in Northern Ireland could remember seeing before, though something like it had happened more than once in the nineteenth century. Against a backdrop of blazing buildings, small groups of exhausted policemen huddled in doorways or lay in the streets, their faces streaked with blood and dirt, their tunics torn and even burned, like the weary survivors of some desperate and costly offensive.

These images began to flicker round the world. In Belfast, diversionary attacks were made upon the police to prevent reinforcements being sent to Derry. Firing broke out in republican areas of the city. The police replied with sub-machineguns. A child was killed when a bullet came through the wall of his home. The disorders spread all over the province. The Government of Northern Ireland was obliged to ask for the assistance of the army. On every previous occasion the army had acted in aid of the civil power, but this time Westminster acceded to the request only on condition that political control was taken out of the hands of the local government. Thus began the crisis in Ulster.

Everyone knows that these two episodes of Ulster history are connected. But in what way? To people whose history stays flat on the printed page it seems incredible that 'old, far-off, unhappy things, and battles long ago' should exert such influence upon the present. Is it true that the Irish are obsessed by their history? And what is the nature of the influence which the past exerts upon them? Ireland, like Dracula's Transylvania, is much troubled by the undead. King William III, Wolfe Tone and Patrick Pearse sustain an unnatural immortality with the blood of succeeding generations, and when people talk about the inability of the Irish to forget the past, this is usually what they mean. As a matter of fact, the Irish are not only capable of forgetting the past, but quite deliberately expunge from their minds whole areas of it. Like other nations, they have woven for themselves a garment of myth and legend which they call Irish history. Having designed it themselves, they have taken great care to make it as comfortable as possible, eliminating the loose threads and sharp edges, and making it so snug and warm that when they are wearing it they sometimes imagine themselves to be immune to the ordinary dictates of humanity. Moreover, it exports extremely well, and has been sold in every country in the world. The general opinion is that it is a superb article and well worth the price.

The price is high. To the Irish all History is Applied History, and the past is simply a convenient quarry which provides ammunition to use against enemies in the present. They have little interest in it for its own sake. So when we say that the Irish are too much influenced by the past, we really mean that they are too much influenced by Irish history, which is a different matter. That is the history they learn at their mother's knee, in school, in books and plays, on radio and television, in songs and ballads. But they are influenced in another way by the past, as everyone is, and since they are often quite unconscious of this kind of influence, it is rarely discussed. It is with the second kind of subjection to the past that this book is chiefly concerned.

At an early stage of the Ulster troubles, it became apparent that attitudes, words and actions which were familiar and recognizable to any student of Irish history, but which seemed hardly relevant to politics in the twentieth century, were coming back into fashion. This was not to be explained by the deliberate imitation of the past; it could be accounted for only by some more mysterious form of transmission from generation to generation. In many ways it was a frightening revelation, a nightmarish illustration of the folk-memory of Jungian psychology. Men and women who had grown to maturity in a Northern Ireland at peace now saw for the first time the monsters which inhabited the depths of the community's unconscious mind. It was as if a storm at sea had brought to the surface creatures thought to have been long extinct.

The metaphor is appropriate. For most of our lives we see only the surface of our society, as a man strolling on a marine promenade sees only a calm and uniform expanse of water. But in certain lights he will discern the meandering streams which traverse the sea as they do the land. He does not know from whence they come, or what determines their course. He cannot see the foul ground, the towering mountains and drowned valleys, the dark currents scouring the headlands, or the intricate ebb and flow in the sound where the tides meet.

The historian likes to think of himself as an oceanographer rather than a stroller on the promenade. He prepares his charts of the past from precise data, the most accurate he can obtain. But he labours under many disadvantages. Not only does his discipline usually concern itself with limited and carefully defined questions; it requires him to use only one kind of evidence in finding the answers. It may be that written evidence does not contain the answer, and even that the determinant factors had already operated before any records were kept.

Nevertheless, there are times when he can read between the lines of his written record, and try to provide his own response

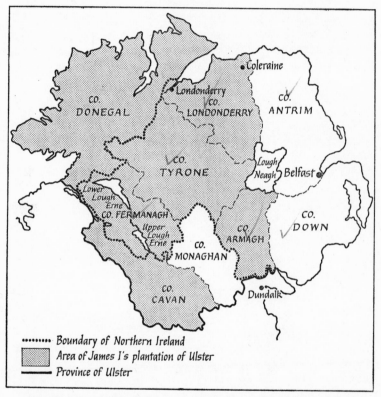

1 Map of the Ulster Plantation and the present Northern Ireland

to Prospero's question, 'What see'st thou else in the dark backward and abysm of Time?' Like the aerial archaeologist, or the Lough Neagh fisherman of Ulster legend, he may glimpse the distinctive patterns of the past below the surface. It is with the shape of the past, rather than its surface details, that this study is concerned.

PART ONE

Problems of Plantation

# 1. Planter and Gael

Few episodes in Irish history have been more misunderstood, or more misrepresented, than the Plantation of Ulster. Of all the factors needed to provide an explanation of the present situation, it is generally considered to be the chief; and Irishmen, whatever their political attitudes, are agreed at least on one point—that the Ulster Question began in 1609. Everyone else believes it too. Contrite Scotsmen even write to the Belfast newspapers, begging forgiveness for the consequences of James VI and I's disastrous intervention in Ireland's affairs. Every bullet fired and every bomb exploded in Northern Ireland is laid to the blame of a monarch dead these three centuries. For the historian, however, nothing can ever be as simple as this.

There is no lack of documentary evidence for the Plantation of Ulster, but the documents at the same time tell us too much and too little. The sheer weight of written evidence assures the whole episode of a secure place in the history books when other equally important developments are left out. This is in itself a trap when we begin to consider its significance, for historians must give greatest weight to the written record. What they have generally done is to examine the detailed plans for the plantation, the reports of the commissioners, the adulatory accounts of courtiers, and the many surveys and inquisitions, and to assume that they describe the plantation as it actually occurred. But we know even from the evidence of the written record itself that in two vital respects the plantation did not proceed as planned: the Irish were not, as is popularly supposed, driven off the escheated lands wholesale; and the Scots eventually occupied an area of the plantation out of all proportion to that originally allotted to them.

Each of these developments requires to be examined in more detail. The first resulted, at least in part, from the planters' failure to keep the terms of their contract with the Crown, and to understand how this occurred we must be more specific about what

actually happened in James I's reign. The Tudor conquest of
Ireland was not completed until a few days after the death of
Elizabeth, when on 30 March 1603 Hugh O'Neill surrendered to
her deputy, Mountjoy. Ulster, the heart of O'Neill's territory, at
last lay open to English supremacy. The division into counties,
first projected in 1585, was now put into effect. English law took
the place of Irish, a class of Irish freeholders dependent on the
Crown balanced the former power of the chieftains, and the Earls
of Tyrone and Tyrconnell were given back their lands, but now
as tenants-in-chief of the Crown.

The next logical step was the resumption of a policy of plantation which had been abandoned during the Elizabethan wars. In
1605 the Lord Deputy, Sir Arthur Chichester, proposed the
settlement of English and Scots in certain areas to strengthen
royal control of the province, and in the next year he proposed
a scheme for the whole county of Cavan, in which the new settlers
were to obtain land without dispossessing the Irish. When Tyrone
and Tyrconnell suddenly fled from Ireland to the Continent in
1607, the way was open for a much more comprehensive plan.
The flight of the earls was taken as evidence of their treason, their
estates were forfeited to the Crown, and the King reversed his
earlier policy by asserting a claim to confiscate the whole area over
which the earls had wielded authority. Six of the nine new Ulster
counties were escheated to the Crown, those of Armagh, Cavan,
Coleraine (later Londonderry), Donegal, Fermanagh and Tyrone.
Chichester at once seized the opportunity to put before the English
Privy Council a detailed scheme for the colonization of these
counties, in which once more the Irish proprietors were to be
allowed first to take as much land as they could develop before the
introduction of English and Scots.

At this point Sir Cahir O'Doherty of Inishowen unexpectedly
broke into rebellion to avenge an insult by the Governor of Derry.
In April 1608 he seized the fort at Culmore on the shores of
Lough Foyle and then captured and sacked Derry. His rebellion,
which had little support outside his own territory, was swiftly
crushed and he himself was killed in July; but its result was the end
of official support for Chichester's ideas for the favourable treatment of Irish landholders. The comprehensive scheme of plan-

tation, published in 1609 and modified in 1610, set aside only a
small area of each county for 'deserving' natives. The rest, apart
from lands granted to the Church, was to be settled with English
and Scottish planters.

Under the original scheme all those to whom the land was
regranted were divided into three categories. The first, and most
important, consisted of 'undertakers' who were given large areas
to be held of the Crown in socage, and who agreed to settle on their
lands Protestant English and 'inland Scottish' farmers, husband-
men, artificers and cottagers. They were to establish villages, build
fortified farmhouses called 'bawns' and keep arms for the defence
of the settlement. The second category, of 'servitors', held their
lands on less favourable terms, but unlike the undertakers they
were permitted to take Irish tenants. Lastly came the Irish proprietors who were also allowed to take Irish tenants. They held
their estates in fee farm and paid much higher rents than the undertakers, though they were bound by the same obligation to build
and defend castles, houses and bawns. In addition to this scheme,
the entire county of Coleraine was granted to twelve London companies to develop. The area included the rich fisheries of the
rivers Bann and Foyle. In return for these privileges, the companies
were to exclude the Irish as tenants, to levy twenty thousand
pounds for the plantation, and to rebuild and fortify the towns of
Derry and Coleraine. The companies were considered more capable
of defending the coastline than any single planter, and were therefore granted 'the office of Admiralty', that is, the jurisdiction and
profits of the coasts of Donegal and Coleraine. The town of Derry
was renamed Londonderry and the same name was given to the
county of Coleraine.

The fact that the Catholic population of Ireland today will not
use the 'London' part of this name is in itself indicative of the
significance attached to these arrangements. The general opinion
is that the Ulster plantation added a new and unassimilable element to the Irish population, and that the beginning of the 'Ulster
problem' can be precisely fixed in the second decade of the seventeenth century. From that point on, the population was sharply
divided into planters and Gaels, and this division is still preserved in
the political divisions of today. The planters, it is argued, changed

the face of Ulster by the end of the seventeenth century, building
the plantation towns, clearing the woodlands and replacing the Irish
pastoral habits with intensive cultivation. A thriving and indust-
rious community with the Puritan ethic that hard work was a virtue,
they laid the foundations of Ulster's future industrial development, and also of the partition of Ireland in the twentieth century.

There can be no doubt of the intensity of Irish feeling on this
subject. Nationalist historical writing on the plantation is often
tinged with bitter sarcasm for the character of the early settlers as
revealed by their own accounts, and enormous labour has been
expended to uncover every detail of the undoubted legal chicanery
by which most of the former proprietors were deprived of their
lands. The settlers are regarded as a completely alien race, a
permanent garrison planted only to ensure the success of British
policy in Ireland and to impose a different culture and civilization
on the region. Moreover they reduced the proud and freedom-
loving Gaels to the status of 'hewers of wood and drawers of
water' and kept them in that condition until the present. There is
always an implication that this situation cannot really be ended
until the descendants of the settlers either leave Ireland or change
their politics. The Ulster Protestants, for their part, though not so
much given to writing history, have built up a mystique which
exactly complements the nationalist view, a conception of the
Ulster Scots as a naturally superior race, tough, loyal and self-
reliant, easily distinguishable from the Catholic Irish and free of
all their more obvious vices.

The distinction between planter and Gael is thus popularly
supposed to derive from history. What was the distinction? The
terms are freely used by poets to indicate separate cultural traditions, but historians must use them with greater caution. Let us
look first at the question of population. Neither the undertakers nor
the London companies found it expedient or possible to clear all
the native Irish from their lands, and therefore they accepted
them as tenants, violating their contracts with the Crown in order
to do so. Without the Irish tenants it is doubtful whether the Scots
and English planters would have made even such limited progress
as they had by 1641. The great concealed factor in this whole
'British' plantation is the part played by the relatively undisturbed

Irish population in building the towns, fortified bawns and planter castles, and in developing the resources of forests, rivers and loughs. In practice, it proved very difficult to persuade English and Scots to take up lands under the plantation scheme, and the evidence that the undertakers did not fulfil their contracts is very extensive.[1] When we remember that the servitors and Irish grantees were actually permitted to take Irish tenants, it becomes clear beyond doubt that a very substantial proportion of the original population was not disturbed at all. Modern historical research on the plantation has thrown much light on this continuity of actual population.[2]

The matter is not, of course, as simple as that. The plantation began processes which did, in the long run, cause the Catholic population of Ulster to be concentrated in the least fertile areas, and some attempt will be made later to explain these processes. But as far as actual expulsion of population is concerned, the reality was not as it is so often presented in the poet's lament for the Gael, driven off the fertile land of his fathers and forced to take refuge in the mountain fastnesses. There were many Gaelic lords whose lands were confiscated (though it would be more accurate to say that they lost their status because a new system was imposed on the one by which they lived). Frequently they became outlaws, and, with the followers who remained loyal to them, established themselves in inaccessible areas from which they raided the plantation. They nurtured a desire for revenge, and on many occasions before 1641 created a considerable threat to the settlers. These men show up clearly in plantation records and in such sources as the Calendars of State Papers. The lament of the Gael was *their* lament, the poets were *their* poets.

It is therefore necessary to keep in mind a distinction between the dispossessed landowners as such, with their deep sense of grievance, and the entire pre-plantation population. The sharp line of division was one of religion, not of race. The evidence of family names would suggest that since 1609 many Gaels have become Protestants and 'British' by the same process of assimilation which more frequently has operated in the reverse direction. Hence those surnames of obviously Irish origin which are in modern Ulster recognized by the locals as distinctively Protestant, and which are not commonly found in Britain. And not all of the planters were Protestant, as is popularly supposed, thus adding another complicating element to the mosaic of settlement.[3]

From the very outset, however, religion provides the vital distinction. The dispossessed did not give up their faith. They clung to it the more tenaciously as the badge of their former status and the explanation of their unjust deprivation. It was the priests who nourished their dreams of re-possession and identified their plight with that of a threatened and persecuted Church. This was already an old pattern, established in the preceding century, one to which they naturally and easily reverted, and one which was to persist for the future. Already in Henry VIII's reign the dispossessed chieftains were identifying their hatred for the new planter with the defence of their faith and their Church, and we find Pope Paul III writing letters to Con O'Neill to deplore the sufferings of Ireland at the hands of her neighbour and to acknowledge with gratitude his defence of the Catholic faith.[4] It is a pattern which has not changed even marginally (in spite of much talk to the contrary) in four centuries.

In what has gone before we have used 'Irish' as an easily identifiable term to describe the population at a point just before the plantation took place, but it needs a finer definition. We may swiftly dispose of the question of race. The theory of a racial distinction between planter and 'Gael', though it still dominates Irish thinking on the subject, can no longer be sustained. The heyday of the belief that the Irish and the 'British' were separate races, as well as separate nations, occurred towards the end of the nineteenth century, when the scientific investigation of racial types became fashionable, producing much learned debate and a plethora of books. This was the time when the Gaelic revival took place in Ireland, and the belief was fostered that there had been a 'pure' Gaelic race before the Saxon invaders had come. The expatriate Irish in America and Australia began to talk about 'the Irish race', and the term is still current in some circles. The Ulster unionists also talked about race, and particularly cherished Lord Rosebery's tribute to the Ulster Scots. 'They are, I believe, without exception the toughest, the most dominant, the most irresistible race that exists in the universe at this moment.'[5]

Such racial theories have not stood up well to more scientific investigation in the twentieth century, and they became more than unpopular when they were taken up by Adolf Hitler and the Nazis in Germany. Even the discussion of race has since become repugnant to educated opinion, but such inconvenient changes of intellectual fashion are little heeded in Ireland, and though the Irish may no longer say so, they clearly still *believe* in racial identity. In an island which was the terminus for so many westward-moving waves of population throughout the ages, the idea of an unmixed racial group ought to have been laughed out of court at the outset. But the Irish nation of today has derived its knowledge of these matters more from the treasury of Gaelic literature than from scientific textbooks. The emotion of nationalism is intense, and when it is coincident with religion, and admiration for a particular culture, it is unshakeable.

Such modern scientific investigation of the subject as there has been (and it is perhaps less than one might assume) points to results startlingly divergent from the popular view. The question 'Who are the Irish?' is not an easy one to answer. 'A pure race is a nationalist myth,' writes Professor E. E. Evans; 'indeed it is now thought that in the evolution of man the mixed breeds were the winners from the start. We are all mongrels, and should be proud of it, but the proportions of the various racial elements in the mixture vary from one region to another. From sampling, it appears that 88 per cent of the Irish have light eyes (including blue-brown); but it is strangely combined with dark hair. This is the prevailing Irish type, but there are many other strains. The darkest hair, by the way, is found in Wexford and Waterford. Many stereotypes about Irish racial characters derive from nineteenth-century theories. It used to be stated that the taller fair-haired types predominate in Ulster and down the English-settled east coast, where the conquering Nords entered, the little dark folk, those dangerous emotional "Iberians", predominating in the Gaelic-speaking west. In fact the mean stature of the Irish people is lowest on the east coast and highest in Kerry and Galway. The heaviest men are found in the westernmost peninsulas, and the broadest heads in Co. Kerry. These are probably relics of an ancient strain of Irishmen who took refuge there. Most paradoxical is the physical make-up of the men of Aran, one of the strongest bulwarks of Gaelic culture. Studies of both racial characters and blood-group ratios suggest that they owe much to the infusion of the blood of Cromwellian soldiers, who were recruited from the English Fenlands. But Ireland has completely absorbed them.'[6]

Evidence of this kind may be challenged or revised from time to time, but it is unlikely that the general inference will be shaken. The demonstration that the Irish are a mixture of many European strains is in no way inimical to aspirations of nationhood, any more than it is for the English or Scots. How could it be otherwise? And it must be emphasized that the mixing does not begin with the recorded incursions of historical times; it begins in prehistory, for the Gaels themselves were invaders who became in time *hiberniciores hibernicis ipsis*. Professor Evans has argued that the Irishness of the Irish goes back to the first Neolithic peoples in the island, and the testimony of the spade gives striking corroboration of this view—almost literally so, for it is in agriculture and its implements that he found some of the most significant clues. During the last thirty or forty years archaeologists have been patiently unveiling the truth about Ireland's earliest culture, the surprisingly sophisticated and stable culture of the megalith-builders. Only a few decades ago little was known of them except the great stone monuments they left; now 'hundreds of megalithic sites which have been studied and classified tell us that a peasant culture deeply concerned with religious ideas, with votive offerings and magic ceremonies at wells, in lakes and on hill-tops, was already established in nearly every part of Ireland well before 2,000 B.C.'[7]

The most striking aspect of all the subsequent invasions of Ireland is that they created ruling minorities. The original population was never exterminated or replaced: it assimilated its conquerors. There was nowhere it could be driven to except the Atlantic, and this was one of the ways in which 'Irishness' was in fact determined by geography. The markedly un-Gaelic physical characteristics of the people now living in the Irish-speaking areas of the south and west point clearly to the conclusion that the bogs and mountains were sanctuaries for more than one supplanted culture, the last and most easily identifiable being Gaelic. For the Gaels, too, were invaders, a military caste ruling the native population every bit as much as the later Normans or English. In the nineteenth century, and for much later, it was assumed that the Gaels must have been the earliest Celtic speakers to arrive in Ireland. Thomas O'Rahilly's *Early Irish History and Mythology*, a pioneer work published in 1946, argued that they were in reality the last of *four* distinct waves of invasion. The term 'Celtic' is a linguistic one and cannot properly be related to race: the Gaels were anthropologically very mixed. Yet one still hears the Irish described as 'a Celtic race'. The point is that the language became a unifying agent: it was eventually adopted by a collection of dwellers in Ireland, people of different origins fused by a conquering culture. Much later it was to be learned by invaders of Gaelic Ireland who came speaking Norse, French, English and Welsh, and an Irishman who speaks it today might easily be, and indeed probably is, the descendant of Normans or English or Scots.

Consider for a moment the obstacles which would have to be overcome in order to believe that the true Irish today are descended from a pure Celtic race. We would have to believe that invaders of this race entirely subjugated Ireland, exterminating the population already established there for more than five thousand years, and that it remained completely uncontaminated by the blood of the Vikings, the Normans, the Old English, Old Welsh and Old Scots, the settlers of the sixteenth- and seventeenth-century plantations, the Cromwellian soldiers, the English and Scots who came in during the eighteenth century, and, not least, the enormous casual movement of population from 1800 and especially in fairly recent times.

It is not difficult to see why a simpler idea of a pure ethnic nation of Gaels became accepted as history and made its way into the national consciousness. The Gaels were dominant for a long time, and they left a rich literature on which all the historical superstructure has hitherto rested. It is only recently that this superstructure has had to yield to new scientific techniques and to new methods in archaeology, in the study of folklore, dialect, crafts and customs.

The first inhabitants of Ulster, whoever they were, were not the
Gaels. Nor were they the Ulaid, who gave the region its name.
The earliest recognizable concept of Ulster is the *cóiced n Ulaid*,
literally the province of the Ulaid. It goes back to the first centuries A.D. and perhaps earlier. The capital of the Ulaid is traditionally supposed to be Emain Macha, close to the city of Armagh.
The great mound there has been very carefully excavated by
archaeologists in recent years. It did not yield any dramatic
evidence to confirm or refute this assumption, but proved beyond
doubt that beneath it lay a settlement two thousand years older.
In the same way, at the hill of Tara, in the Boyne valley, archaeologists have been able to show that the site had been sacred to the
natives for two thousand years before the Celtic fortress was built
upon it. Queen Macha was almost certainly not a Celtic queen but
a much older goddess.[8]

Nor were the Ulaid the first Celtic-speakers to settle in Ulster,
for O'Rahilly considers that they belonged to the second of his
four migrations. They were conquerors, like so many of their
successors, and within their territory remained scattered communities of Pretani, from the first Celtic migration (in Irish they
were called the Cruthin). The Pretani, though largely submerged
in Ireland, remained dominant in Scotland, where from the third
century A.D. they emerge as those old friends of our schooldays,
the Picts. In Ulster pockets of Pretani can be identified in Co.
Antrim (Dalriada), in the west of Co. Down, and possibly in the
Ards Peninsula. The Gaels, as we have said, belonged to the last
of the Celtic-speaking migrations. In the fifth century A.D. a
section of the Gaels who had settled in Tara, the Ui Néill, invaded
the Ulaid territory to the north. The Ulaid were defeated and
their capital at Emain Macha was destroyed. As a result the
chieftains of the Ui Néill settled their followers in the middle and
western parts of Ulster, and they established there the dominant
culture until the defeat of the great Hugh O'Neill in 1603.

## 2. The Old Plantation

It is often said that at the end of Elizabeth's reign Ulster was the most Gaelic of the four provinces. The statement is true but misleading. What it means is that English influence and authority had made less progress in Ulster than in any of the other provinces. Its impenetrable woods and surrounding mountains shielded the power base of the O'Neills in the central area of Tyrone, and insulated the province as a whole from the influences emanating from the Pale, including that of the English Reformation. But it is after all a relative statement and it is frequently misinterpreted to mean that until 1603 Ulster had been immune from English and Scots colonization. Nothing could be further from the truth. Behind James I's 'New Plantation in Ulster' lay an old plantation of considerable antiquity, and one which was still in operation when he ascended the throne. Irish historians have played down or ignored this plantation with the result that many of its most obvious consequences have been attributed to other and more recent causes.

By 1603, at least the eastern seaboard, and probably a great deal more of the eastern half of the province, had undergone a long history of colonization, of which only the barest written record survives. Its existence is much more obvious to the archaeologist than to the historian, and is indeed still apparent to the eye of any interested observer of the countryside. We can easily forget that the Gaelic O'Neills were as much foreigners in Ulster as the Scots who later took their lands from them. Nor can the period between the coming of the O'Neills and the Tudor and Stuart plantations be seen as one long pastoral idyll of contented Gaels raising sheep and cattle on the Ulster uplands until their expulsion by the Saxon and the Scot. The already thoroughly mixed population which existed at the beginning of historic times had to absorb wave after wave of new invaders. To it we must add the Vikings, who in the ninth century established a great many colonies in eastern Ireland

and gave Ireland its first towns. The placenames of eastern Ulster provide plenty of evidence of their settlements and influence—Strangford and Carlingford loughs, islands and reefs with names like the Skerries or Skullmartin (from *skyr* meaning reef). After the Norse came the Anglo-Normans, who have left still clearer evidence of settlement. Many of their castles, churches and monasteries still stand, and even more surprisingly the scores of motte and bailey sites are still unobliterated, including even some within the city of Belfast itself.

In 1177 John de Courcy left Dublin with twenty-two knights and three hundred followers and overran the ancient Ulaid kingdom of East Ulster. He secured the coastline and then pushed inland as far to the west as Tyrone, subsequently styling himself *princeps Ultoniae*. De Courcy acted on his own initiative: he was never created Earl of Ulster, and his effective sway was probably confined to the area of Antrim and Down. He consolidated his position by marrying the daughter of Godred, King of Man and Lord of the Isles, but in 1205 his power was taken away by King John who granted the earldom of Ulster (*totam terram Ultoniae*) to Hugh de Lacy. The Anglo-Norman colony which de Courcy founded extended along the south-eastern coast of Co. Down to connect with the Pale, and its heart was Lecale, the area to the south-west of Strangford almost isolated by marshlands from the rest of the Ulster mainland. There is extensive evidence of close Anglo-Norman settlement in the two peninsulas of Lecale and Ards which together encircle Strangford Lough. The archaeologist and the local historian who turn their attention to these areas can have no doubt that it was a highly developed and well-organized colony. The evidence is of course also tantalizing; it does not tell the expert enough about the manorial organization or the precise methods of agriculture, nor does it tell him whether the farmers were settlers or the original population. He can only say that, for example, some parts of East Down were being profitably farmed within a generation of de Courcy's invasion, or that the distribution of mottes reflects the degree of penetration of Anglo-Norman authority in the century after 1177.

That power was broken by the incursions of Edward Bruce in 1314–18, but for a long time before then the line dividing the

Gaelic chieftains from the Anglo-Norman vassals of English kings had been misty. In 1264, for example, the earldom passed into the hands of the de Burgos, the powerful Norman family long established in Galway, and already half-gaelicized. After the Bruce invasion the Anglo-Norman grip on eastern Ulster weakened, and for the next three centuries was confined to a few isolated pockets on the coastal fringes of Down. The Irish crept eastwards again to re-occupy even the strongest of the Norman castles, such as Dundrum, and the old colony was submerged. But though the earldom soon ceased to exist as a political entity, the settlement survived through the centuries, and the planted families in Ards and Lecale clung tenaciously to their lands, even becoming Gaelic and 'Irish' in order to do so. By Tudor times they were already officially described as 'degenerate' English. But they kept their names, which are still preserved in association with scores of sites—Hackett, Jordan, Audley, Russell, White and Savage. The Savages of Upper Ards were almost the only Anglo-Norman family to survive as landowners through the sixteenth century, and in 1536 Roland Savage was accounted as an Irish chieftain. An Elizabethan poet wrote of

> *The Ards of Uladh ...*
> *Where Savage hath, nor bread, nor herds, nor flocks,*
> *But lives by scraping limpets off the rocks.*[9]

Almost certainly the Anglo-Norman colony had a greater significance in the shaping of East Ulster than is generally assumed. At the very least it meant that the eastern fringes of Ulster had experienced extensive and determined 'English' settlement before the seventeenth century.

In addition to all this, with its implications for the mixture of population, we have to consider the very determined efforts at English colonization in Ulster during the sixteenth century. These are generally held to have failed for one reason or another. For example, the attempts at plantation in parts of Counties Monaghan, Armagh, Down and Antrim in the 1570s were all frustrated by the O'Neills of Tyrone and Clandeboye and the MacDonnells of Antrim. The attempts of Sir Thomas Smith in 1571 and 1574 to create an English settlement in the Ards peninsula,

with a walled city to be called *Elizabetha*, and of the Earl of
Essex to make a similar settlement in Antrim, came to little; but
the 'Enterprise of Ulster', as it was called, was a significant contri-
bution to contemporary colonial theory, and bore fruit in the
colonization of both Virginia and Massachusetts, and in the
Jacobean plantation of Ulster which so overshadows it.[10]

# 3. A Scottish Dimension

Complicated as this lamination of cultures may seem, it still leaves
out of account the most important element of all. At the core of the
Ulster problem is the problem of the Scots, and it requires to be
considered on its own. It is far too often assumed that it began
only in the reign of James I. In fact it was by then already centuries
old. At the narrowest part of the North Channel, Scotland is a
mere twelve miles from the Antrim coast. From the time of the
earliest human occupation of the region this proximity has been
the cause of migration in both directions. It is now generally
accepted that the Early Mesolithic people who were Ireland's
first inhabitants arrived by this route. Of the many later migrations one of the most important was that which occurred in the
second half of the fifth century, a migration of the gaelicized
Ulaid into Argyll. We usually think of eastern Ulster as an extension of Scotland, but it is just as true that western Scotland was
once an extension of the Ulster kingdom of Dalriada. The mediaeval Latin word for Irishman was *Scotus* and these emigrants
actually 'gave Scotland her name, her first kings, her Gaelic
language and her faith'.[11] Some at least of the planters who arrived
in Ulster in the early seventeenth century were direct descendants
of earlier Ulster invaders of Scotland.

Even to use the terms 'Irish' and 'Scots' in this context creates
a misunderstanding. We are talking of a time before the emergence
of the modern idea of a nation or a country. The words have no
meaning beyond a geographical one. Nor can we even think in
terms of natural boundaries determined by the sea. We have

accepted those boundaries as natural for so long that we can easily forget that mountains, forests and marshes were at one time greater obstacles to man than the open sea. The Dutch geographer, Professor Heslinga, argues that from prehistoric times the Irish Sea had been the *centre*, not the frontier, of a vast cultural province.[12] It is here that the historian needs to see the problem through a geographer's eyes. He has to forget his concept of national frontiers and think instead of Highland and Lowland Zones of Britain, and of the so-called thalassocracies, sea-realms with ill-defined frontiers but a strong internal structure of sea-routes. The early connection between Scotland and the north of Ireland is not explicable in any other terms, and it is not very useful to talk about 'Scottish' influence in Ireland in these early centuries.

After the Norman conquest of England, however, the separate identity of Scotland and Ireland becomes clearer, though a long time will still have to elapse before the peoples of these areas will feel the power of centralized government or any sense of unity. We may therefore consider the post-mediaeval colonies in a rather different light. There was in fact a much earlier effective Scots plantation in Antrim than that which began in the first decade of the seventeenth century. Many histories simply do not mention it at all, while others devote to it only a few lines or even a single vague reference to the MacDonnells. Heslinga argues that this is because anti-partitionists fear that to admit the existence of an earlier Scots colony might tend to buttress the Unionist case in terms of propaganda, although its most obvious consequence has been the survival of a Catholic and staunchly nationalist enclave in north Antrim. This Catholic bridgehead in the very heartland of Protestant territory is (like the corresponding enclave in South Down) an embarrassment to unionists and a strong card in the hands of anti-partitionists.[13] It is yet another of those strange anomalies in the Ulster situation which are often not perceived by outside 'authorities' on the problem.

Whatever the reason may be, the history of the first Scots colony remains largely a blank page. A great deal of research has still to be done before it can be written. Until we know much more about it, it will not be possible to assert that the post-1606 immigration is alone responsible for shaping the distinctive culture of the Ulster Scot. The first wave of this settlement began in the thirteenth century, with the migration from the Western Isles and the Highlands of Scots mercenary soldiers. These 'gallowglass', as they were called, were drawn over by the Irish chieftains who employed them in their own feuds and sometimes rewarded them with land. Many of the gallowglass settled in Ulster and were in time assimilated by Irish society as the Normans had been before them. In 1399 the heiress of the Norman lordship in eastern Antrim married John Mor MacDonnell, the Lord of the Isles. The son of this union became Lord of Antrim and Lord of the Isles; thus Antrim was absorbed in the MacDonnell kingdom, a development opposed neither by the English power in Ireland nor by the Earls of Ulster. The combined lordship lasted throughout the fifteenth century, resisting the hostility of the Scottish kings until the Scottish part was overrun and the MacDonnells defeated by James IV. The MacDonnells were left with only Islay and some of the smaller islands, and the political centre of the lordship moved across to Antrim, where huge numbers of the Islanders took refuge. In 1550 James MacDonnell, still calling himself Lord of the Isles, and able to command ten thousand Hebridean Scots ('Redshanks'), was pushing the O'Neills of Clandeboye off their lands to the south and west.

For nearly two centuries, therefore, the MacDonnell lordship had been the link between Gaelic Scotland and Gaelic Ireland, and embedded somewhere in this largely undiscussed history lies the explanation of the Scots Gaelic spoken in Ulster until the plantation, a language distinct in many ways from Irish Gaelic. During this whole period many permanent Scottish settlements were made on the Antrim coast. The Scots intermarried with the Irish, took part in their internecine feuds, and sided with them against the English.

They were regarded as a formidable menace to the further extension of English authority in Ulster. It was difficult enough to deal with the wild Irish, without having to worry about 'wild Scotch' in Ireland as well. The volumes of State Papers for the reign of Henry VIII abound with references to the encroachment and settlement of the Scots in Antrim, and in Mary's reign Parliament passed legislation to prevent the 'bringing in of Scots, retaining them and marrying with them'.[14] By this act it became a felony for anyone in Ireland to marry a Scot who was not already a denizen of Ulster.

During Elizabeth's reign, the official attitude alternated between grudging recognition of the MacDonnell position in Antrim and sporadic attempts to weaken it, either by projected plantation or by allowing Shane O'Neill to lead forays against them, as he did after his submission to the Queen in 1563. The Scots had their revenge, however, by murdering Shane and releasing their captured chieftain Sorley Boy MacDonnell. Thereafter colonization appeared to the government to be the best way of dealing with the Scots problem, but the failure of the plantation schemes of the 1570s left the MacDonnells more securely established than ever.

The policy of keeping the Scots out of Ulster was dramatically reversed by James I. Now for the first time the Crown, and the Scot who was to be kept out, were one. To the Tudor sovereigns the Scots in Ulster had been only a threat; now they became a positive asset. James's policy towards Scottish settlement in Ulster long predated his accession to the throne of England in 1603, and was bound up with the gradual extension of his royal authority to the north-western areas of Scotland. Several factors now combined to make plantation more feasible, and the quickening of interest in the colonization of underpopulated lands occurred at a time when conditions in Ulster were at last favourable to settlement.

The Scots, with the encouragement and favour of their royal compatriot, provided a substantial proportion of the original undertakers and their tenants in the Plantation of Ulster proper. But the actual extent of their colonizing influence was much greater than this, for, even before the larger plantation was projected, a new Scottish colony was established in Antrim and Down. This colony was permanent, and decisive in terms of population; it not only securely buttressed the wider plantation, which would otherwise probably have failed, but gave it its distinctively Scottish character, so that the English aspect of the plantation, which was to have been all-important, was in time to be overshadowed, though never completely overwhelmed.

When James succeeded to the English throne in 1603, Hugh Montgomery, the laird of Braidstane in Ayr, already had his eyes on the lands of Con O'Neill in North Down. O'Neill had rebelled in 1601 and had been thrown in prison by Sir Arthur Chichester, the Lord Deputy. Montgomery cleverly organized O'Neill's escape from Carrickfergus Castle and brought him to Scotland, where he offered to obtain a pardon for him from the King in return for a half share of his lands in Upper Clandeboye and the Great Ards. Montgomery travelled to London, and, with the help of his brother, set about fulfilling his part of the bargain. At this point James Hamilton, a former schoolmaster and Scottish adventurer in Ireland, somehow managed to persuade James that O'Neill's lands should be divided into three, a third for himself, a third for Montgomery and a third for O'Neill. The final division was not actually as simple as this suggests. The land was divided in a complicated fashion, to ensure that the strategic coastal areas were populated by Scots. The two adventurers extended their territories by some very dubious means, and in the end Hamilton succeeded in buying out most of O'Neill's share.

The beginning of the Hamilton–Montgomery plantation in the Ards peninsula in 1606 was hardly auspicious. The first planters from the Lowlands of Scotland did not wrest a fertile, cultivated and populous region from Gaelic proprietors. They came instead to a country devastated by war and famine, where they had to struggle to survive the first winter, as the Puritan Fathers were to do in New Plymouth a few years later. *The Montgomery Manuscripts* contain a concise and often quoted passage which evokes the stark reality of the first settlement. 'Therefore let us now pause awhile, and we shall wonder how this plantation advanced itself (especially in and about the towns of Donaghadee and Newtown) considering that in the springtime, Ao. 1606, those parishes were now more wasted than America (when the Spaniards landed there) . . . for in all those three parishes aforesaid, thirty cabins could not be found, nor any stone walls, but ruined, roofless churches, and a few vaults at Gray Abbey, and a stump of an old castle in Newtown.'[15]

Yet within two years, aided by good harvests, the planters had transformed the Ards into a garden. The chief reason was undoubtedly the steady stream of Lowland tenants who so quickly filled up the colony and then spread into other areas of the plantation in the north and west. Hamilton and Montgomery succeeded where Sir Thomas Smith failed. They created the bridgehead through which the Scots were to come into Ulster for the rest of the century. It is the eastern Scots plantation, old and new, which is the *real* Plantation of Ulster. It gave the east of the province its peculiar character, and its influence has survived, not because it was the initial stage of the Ulster plantation process, as is almost universally believed, but because of the massive 'concealed' immigration which occurred in the second half of the seventeenth century.

When we try to establish a relationship between the Plantation of Ulster and the existence of Northern Ireland in the twentieth century, we must be aware of certain ambiguities and some imponderable factors. The distinctive Ulster–Scottish culture, isolated from the mainstream of Catholic and Gaelic culture, would appear to have been created not by the specific and artificial plantation of the early seventeenth century, but by the continuous natural influx of Scottish settlers both before and after that episode: in particular, the heavy immigration which took place in the *later* seventeenth century seems to have laid the foundations of the Ulster colony. The presence of the English and Scottish undertakers, important and influential as it was, belongs to a different and more deliberate process, that which created all the other English plantations in Munster and Leinster. It may have been by far the most thorough settlement, and it was clearly intended, like all the other plantations, to secure and consolidate English control of Ireland. In the long run, none of these plantations has proved to be an insuperable barrier to Ireland's achieving a form of political independence from England; they have been assimilable, even in spite of the religious problem.

Immigration from Scotland was fairly continuous for centuries before 1609, and was a fact of geography rather than a fact of history. What happened in the Stuart reigns was that Scots settlers and entrepreneurs seized an opportunity of renewing a migration, which had been temporarily checked, on very advantageous terms. When the response of English settlers

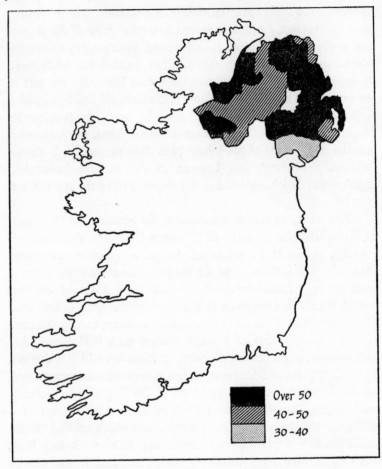

2 Percentage of Protestants in the population of Ireland

Note how the map indicates the two Ulster plantations, east and west. Comparison with a similar map for 1946 shows a decline in Protestant population density in the Irish Republic, and increasing density of Protestant population just inside the border in the west.

fell short of the original intention, and progress in developing the colony was slow, the Scots everywhere took up the slack. Not content with their own portions, they moved into most of the others, including those of the Londonderry plantation. To say this is not to question either the resoluteness, or the defensive hostility towards the native Irish, of the English colonists. The

Scots, and to some extent the Irish themselves, operated within the strong framework of the plantation, taking over the unexploited land and seeking a livelihood by making it productive. The Scots settled in the north from Donegal to Monaghan and Cavan, but they were most densely settled in the eastern half of the plantation.[16] The map of the density of Protestant population in fact reveals two Ulster plantations, one east and one west. The distinction is also indicated in the distribution of the two principal forms of Ulster dialect in English, where the success of the Scots in overrunning the whole north-east of the plantation is clearly apparent. The difference in political attitudes, and in cultural characteristics, between the two plantations is very marked even today, and has some influence on the politics of modern Ulster. Except for Belfast itself, the east is predominantly Protestant whereas the western Protestants are sparsely settled in areas which have a largely Catholic population.

In the eastern half of the plantation, also, the Scots occupied land which had been continuously subjected to organized colonization over many centuries, and in these areas the population had long been a mixture of many strains of 'alien' settlers. There never was any true confrontation of archetypal Planter and Gael. The essentially mixed character of the pre-plantation population has been for so long denied, or deliberately obscured, in the cause of Gaelic nationalism, that it is almost with a shock of new discovery that we find that it was perfectly recognized by contemporaries at the time of the Ulster plantation. Sir John Davies marvelled in 1612 at the continued failure of the English to subdue Ireland since Henry II's reign, 'albeit there have been . . . so many English colonies planted in Ireland, as that, if the people had been numbered this day by the Poll, such as are descended of English race, would be found more in numbers than the Ancient Natives'.[17]

# PART TWO

Signals of Siege

# 1. Sicilian Vespers

Since the settlers of the new plantation were at great pains to distinguish themselves, in religion and nationality if not in race, from the Irish, they found themselves from the very beginning in a state of siege which has continued in one form or another ever since. If it is true that the substructure of Irish tenantry on the planted lands was less disturbed than we are sometimes asked to believe, those who *were* dispossessed, particularly the chieftains and their followers, nourished an undying hostility to the planters, and began at once to plan the recovery of their lands and the exaction of vengeance. This feeling strengthened rather than diminished with time, and was added to the swelling sense of grievance of all the dispossessed Irish, which has given such a legacy of hatred to later generations. It was perpetuated with such intensity that it is still an important aspect of the Ulster problem. It was only since the onset of the recent troubles, after considerable violence and much contentious litigation, that the Catholic fishermen of Lough Neagh won a centuries-old battle against the monopoly of eel fishery granted to patentees in the plantation. Most Catholics believe, and frequently say, that Ireland is 'their' country, not in the usual sense that it is their native land, but in a strictly legal sense—they claim to be the real owners because it was once taken from them.[1] Even in countries which have not long enjoyed political independence, such feelings are rarely so intense or extend so far back in tradition, and they are, of course, quite unknown in Britain. No Englishman, on the dubious ground that he believes himself to be a Saxon, would claim to be the rightful owner of Arundel Castle, or ever say that 'the Normans' had taken it from him.

It is often assumed that the planters remained undisturbed until the rebellion of 1641. This was far from true, and the Calendars of State Papers from 1609 to 1641 provide ample evidence of their alarms and excursions; the castles, bawns and fortified houses were not, after all, built for ornament. The planters inevitably blamed the Catholic clergy, whom they regarded as the fomentors of rebellion. In 1609 we find Chichester complaining that 'priests, who are many' had a powerful hold on the obedience of the Irish, and that the only cause of the latter's continued subjection was 'want of arms, which had all been called in'. There was no lack of men, despite the plague. He feared that the country would ever maintain the title of 'the country of the wild Irish'. In 1611 the redoubtable outlaw Ogie Og O'Hanlon and his followers were terrorizing the British settlers in Armagh. In 1615 there was an unsuccessful plot led by Bryan Crossagh O'Neill and Rory Oge O'Cahan to seize Londonderry, Coleraine, Lifford and Carrickfergus, massacre the new settlers and recover the lands on which they had been planted.[2] In the very heart of the eastern plantation, on Chichester's own lands, there were complaints as late as 1627 of the depredations of 'well-armed and fearless' woodkerne. 'The rebels and kerne in these parts have lately become more mischievous and audacious. They have raided houses close to Lisnagarvey, on Lord Chichester's property, and carried away arms. They were well-armed themselves, and cannot be followed into the woods, where they are well-versed in their beaten haunts. Unless we are protected here we shall be in great danger and be obliged to leave our homes.'[3]

There would probably have been woodkerne in any circumstance; they constituted a perennial Irish problem. But the plantation was chiefly threatened in these years by the supporters of the exiled Gaelic leaders. Upward of five thousand swordsmen were said to be hiding in the woods of Ulster, waiting for a suitable opportunity to attack the plantation. Rumours that the King of Spain would invade Ireland and join forces with the disaffected Irish persisted throughout the reign of James, and became even more credible when Charles became king in 1625, and war with Spain was renewed.

The planters, for their part, brought with them all the mental luggage of sixteenth- and seventeenth-century colonizers. As has often been pointed out, they made little distinction between Ulster and Virginia as a region for colonial development.[4] Neither their attitudes nor their incentives can be understood entirely in the terms of the twentieth century. If King James's motives were determined by policy and strategy, the planters' were largely economic. They migrated to advance their fortunes, and desired simply to bring about the maximum commercial exploitation of the new lands. The process of introducing English laws, customs, speech, habits and dress was the unselfconscious 'civilizing' of Ireland. Why should they have had any twentieth-century reservations on the subject? If the Irish adopted their customs, so much the better; if they continued to cling to their own ways, they remained 'barbarous', 'wild', 'sauvage', 'the king's Irish enemies', 'the meere Irish'. These terms were not simply terms of disparagement, as they now appear to us; they were technical terms. The change in meaning of 'mere' warns us of the treachery of words in conveying to us what contemporaries meant, for 'the mere Irish' signified the pure Irish (Latin *merus*), i.e., those who remained Gaelic in culture and followed the Brehon law. Words like 'civil', 'civility', 'polite' and 'savage' are terms relating to law and governance rather than descriptions of conduct. They were already long established in Anglo-Irish relations when the new planters arrived. So, too, were those technical terms borrowed from the Irish to describe their more striking habits—creaghting (the nomadic pasturing of cattle), bonaght (the quartering of men and horses among the people at large) and coshering (the chieftain's living off his people while on progress through his territory).

The planters were frontiersmen, and naturally displayed frontier attitudes where their lands bordered on those of the native septs. But even more important to them was the problem of the enemy in their midst. From the outset they faced the menace of a fifth column. This was, and still is, the very essence of what is called the Ulster problem. It is not the problem of antagonistic groups confronting each other in different parts of the province; it arises from the mosaic of the settlement itself. The settlers developed over a long time a special kind of siege mentality created by the necessity of having always to test the loyalty of those within the settlement itself, both the 'Irish' settled in pockets within the frontier and those whose steadfastness might have been undermined by constant day by day contact with them, a countercheck to inevitable hibernicization. This is the explanation of one of the more obvious manifestations of the siege outlook, the Lundy fixation. The unfortunate Governor of Derry whose notoriety is so preserved in Protestant mythology was in no sense a traitor, but simply a prudent soldier acting in the interests of the preservation of the people under his care. He has become the archetype of those who would have truck with the enemy; therefore each crisis inevitably produces a new Lundy. It is not an archaic survival but a recurrent nightmate. If Lundy had not existed, it would have been necessary to invent him.

Recurrent siege is thus part of the cycle of the Ulster conflict, a cycle which will continue for a long time to come, whatever the consequences of the recent crisis prove to be. Nationalists argue that this is not so: once Britain relinquishes the north, and the Protestants take their place as an Irish minority, as their co-religionists have done in the south, then the siege mentality will disappear of its own accord. This *may* be true, but it cannot be proved except in the event, and there is no way of showing that the event will not be preceded by an appalling civil war. It rests on the assumption that the northerners feel besieged because they are British and not because they are Protestants. If the spokesmen for Irish nationalism could promise Ulster Protestants that in an Irish Republic they would never again be 'besieged', this would not arrest the process, for in Ireland no one can guarantee that violent men will be or can be controlled, and it is precisely because the most cruel and treacherous warfare has broken out over and over again, and usually after a period of relative security, as in 1641 or 1798 or 1920 or 1969, that the besieged suffer such chronic insecurity. The present conflict has not departed from this pattern.

'If the King of Spain were to land 10,000 men in Ireland,' wrote Lord Carew in 1612, 'all the settlers would be at once massacred, which is not difficult to execute in a moment, by reason they are dispersed, and the native swords will be in their throats in every part of the realm, like the Sicilian Vespers.'[5] His ominous prophecy, in all but the Spanish invasion, was fulfilled thirty years later. The 1641 rebellion is perhaps the most important episode in the history of Ulster since the plantation, yet it is one of the least discussed. Like an unseen planet whose presence is revealed only by its influence on other celestial bodies, the rebellion betrays its significance in later events: the more one explores Ulster history, the more one becomes aware of its occult force. Sooner or later in each successive crisis, the cry is raised of '1641 come again'. The fear which it inspired survives in the Protestant subconscious as the memory of the Penal Laws or the Famine persists in the Catholic.

Though it gave rise to a brisk historical controversy in the late nineteenth century,[6] the rebellion has not received much attention from historians in recent times. The dispute was not so much concerned with the causes and the character of the uprising, as with the extensive massacre of Protestant settlers which was alleged to have occurred in the course of it. The argument turned on whether thirty-two volumes of sworn depositions of eye-witnesses, taken by parliamentary commissioners and now pre-served in the library of Trinity College, Dublin, are to be con-sidered trustworthy evidence. Though conducted within the confines of scholarship, it really followed the sterile course of unionist against nationalist at a time when the home rule agi-tation had caused political feelings to run high. It does not seem credible that such a large body of testimony, with such accurate circumstantial detail in regard to names and places, would have been fabricated simply for the purpose of propaganda. Moreover, evidence is presented equally for the savage retaliatory massacres of Irish Catholics at Islandmagee and elsewhere, though these were on a smaller scale.

On the other hand, the depositions were certainly used for pro-paganda, both at the time and since. As in most accounts of atrocities, there is evidence of exaggeration, and of the super-natural and sexual overtones which made graphic abridgements of the depositions popular reading for later generations. Today it is no longer possible to believe (if it ever was, outside the realms of propaganda) that any section of mankind is more capable of such inhumanity than any other. It does not matter whether these massacres in particular were carried out by Catholics or by Pro-testants. Nor do they reflect upon the Irish as a nation; some of the worst cruelties were attributed to the Scottish followers of the

MacDonnells. That they did occur, however, would seem to be incontrovertible, and their memory has exercised a baneful influence ever since.

If the reluctance of Irish historians in the twentieth century to reopen the old controversies owes something to the feeling that the massacres of 1641 reflect badly on the Catholic and nationalist cause, and strengthen the political attitudes of unionists, it is also to be explained by the daunting complexity of the historical problems involved. The rebellion in Ireland and the troubles in Scotland were a prelude to eleven years of civil war, not only in Ireland but in Britain, where civil war has never been the normal pattern of life. The uprising of the Gaelic Irish in Ulster, though it had specific local causes, has to be related not only to the wider context of Stuart government in the British Isles but to a pattern of war, revolution and atrocity which involved the whole of Europe, and of which the major aspect was the Thirty Years' War. Some historians have seen in it a 'general crisis' of society, just as at the end of the eighteenth century some have discerned a democratic revolution affecting the whole of the Western world.

Irish historians, it may be said in passing, are especially prone to consider the history of Ireland in isolation, as if everything that happened there was the result of a slow process of ferment of purely Irish ingredients, above all of the maturing of a sense of Irish nationality. Irish history is, as it were, seen vertically and not horizontally. Yet nothing can be more obvious than that throughout the centuries the course of events in Ireland has been profoundly influenced by major upheavals in other parts of the world. Thus events in 1641, 1690, 1782, 1798, 1848 and 1916 can all be linked to significant political changes in Europe or America. The prolonged Irish crisis of 1914-23 was coincident in time with the First World War, and events in Northern Ireland since 1969 cannot be dissociated from a worldwide upsurge in terrorism and civil disorder.

In 1641 it was, above all, the tangle of political affairs in England and Scotland which precipitated rebellion. The Irish conspirators from the beginning endeavoured to make Charles I's cause their own, and to represent their attempt to overthrow the Puritan-controlled Irish administration as being no rebellion. Sir Phelim O'Neill took the trouble to forge Charles's instruction to Ulstermen to rise in his defence, and make his followers take an oath of loyalty to the King. Charles's own attitude was not such as to convince the Ulster Scots planters that the commission was in fact forged. At the time, and for long afterwards, they believed that Charles had intended to make the Irish his allies.

In fact Charles was the first to warn the lords justices of the danger of an Irish uprising. When it broke out, he at once dispatched arms for its suppression. Sir Phelim O'Neill, on the scaffold, was offered his life if he could prove that Charles authorized the rising, but he could not, and indeed he admitted the forgery and the reasons for it. Nevertheless the vicissitudes of the long and complex 'war of the three kingdoms' which followed were to create situations in which the king would have been glad of any Irish allies.

The rebellion broke out on 23 October 1641. On the previous day the lords justices had been warned of the plot by the indiscretion of one of the conspirators, and were able to secure the castle and city of Dublin. Significantly perhaps, the news was brought to them by a Catholic turned Presbyterian. In Ulster, however, the rebellion broke out at the time appointed. The simultaneous attack on the scattered planters in many parts of the province took them by surprise. At first people knew only what had happened in their own locality, but as survivors began to straggle into the fortified towns the full horror of the rising gradually became apparent.

Sir Phelim O'Neill treacherously surprised the castle of Charlemont in Armagh while he was the guest of Lord Caulfeild, and then moved to seize Dungannon and Moneymore. In almost every part of the plantation the Irish septs took the field—O'Quins, O'Hanlons, McMahons, O'Reillys—and captured most of the towns and fortified castles. Sir Con Magennis, with the help of the Catholic inhabitants led by Father Crelly, surprised Newry. A few key towns were saved by early warning—Enniskillen, Derry and Lurgan among them—and the garrisons were able to prepare their defence.

At first only the English planters were attacked and the Scots

were left alone, a circumstance which permitted some of them to
flee for safety or prepare to defend themselves. But soon the fury
of the rebels was turned against them also. The scattered settlements of the plantation were overwhelmed one by one, and the
character of the rebellion changed to that of a religious war. The
slaughter of the planters and their families followed, a protracted
St. Bartholomew that continued until the spring of the next year.
The depositions of the survivors tell of men and women butchered
with revolting cruelty, burned alive in churches and farms,
drowned wholesale in rivers, of infants slain before their parents'
eyes, of scores of Protestant clergy put to death, and of refugees
perishing from starvation and exposure. It is not the historical
facts of the rebellion, nor the actual numbers of those slain (which
may be less than is sometimes claimed), but the circumstantial
details of those depositions which have survived in the Protestant
subconscious. Here, if anywhere, the mentality of siege was born,
as the warning bonfires blazed from hilltop to hilltop, and the
beating drums summoned men to the defence of castles and
walled towns crowded with refugees.

## 2. 'That Ominous Place'

'Five generations have passed away,' wrote Macaulay, in a memor-
able sentence, 'and still the wall of Londonderry is to the Protestants of Ulster what the trophy of Marathon was to the Athenians.'[7]
The siege of Londonderry in 1689 was only one of several which
had taken place since the sixteenth century, and it is chiefly
interesting because it provides the paradigm for the entire history
of the siege of the plantation. For that reason it is enshrined in
Protestant tradition, not so much as the record of one event, but as
a set of historical tableaux, what Heslinga aptly calls 'the Derry
cycle',[8] depicting with vivid symbolism the courageous resistance
of the Protestant settlement. The crimson flag which flew from
the Royal Bastion during the siege was the flag both of danger and
of defiance, the hallowed flag which the Apprentice Boys still

carry on their ritual march along the city walls, past the western
gates of the city and of the plantation. The factor which dis-
tinguishes the siege of Derry from all other historic sieges in the
British Isles is that it is still going on.

The siege of Derry began long before the seventeenth century,
and it was made inevitable by the town's strategic situation.
Probably the earliest record of fortifications there is the reference
to the building of a cashel, or circular wall, round the abbey
church in 1162, an operation which required the demolition of
some eighty dwellings. In the reign of Mary Tudor we find the
Lord Deputy, the Earl of Sussex, strongly recommending its
military occupation, but this plan was postponed. In May 1565,
when Elizabeth I was pursuing a strenuous offensive against Shane
O'Neill, the site was occupied by a military force under Colonel
Edward Randolph. Randolph expelled the inhabitants and threw
up earthworks for the defence of the garrison. He was killed at
Muff in 1566 by O'Neill's forces advancing to attack the town,
and in 1567 a fire destroyed the buildings occupied by the troops.
The flames spread to the Temple Mor, or Great Church, which
was being used as a magazine, and caused an explosion. The site
of the Temple is that now occupied by the Long Tower Catholic
church, schools and cemetery. For the next thirty years Derry was
left ungarrisoned, but inevitably the strategic importance of the
Foyle estuary during the wars against the O'Neills and the
O'Donnells re-created the need for a garrison. 'How often,'
Elizabeth inquired of Essex in 1599, 'have you resolved us that
until Loughfoyle and Ballyshannon were planted there could be
no hope of doing service upon the capital rebels?' Essex did not
carry out his commission, however, and bequeathed it to his
successor, Mountjoy, who sent a Yorkshireman, Sir Henry Docwra,
to fortify the town with a force of four thousand foot and two
hundred horse.

Docwra found on his arrival 'a place in manner of an island
comprehending within it 40 acres of ground, wherein were the
ruines of an old Abbey, of a Bishopp's house, of two churches, and
at one of the ends of it an old Castle, the River called loughfoyle
encompassing it all on one side, and a bogg most commonlie wet,
and not easily passable except in two or three places, dividing it

from the maine land'. He immediately erected two forts, one at the riverside and the other on high ground above it. The task was not easy. He took much of his building material from a birch wood

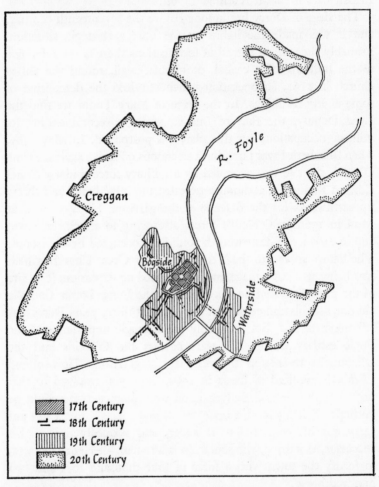

3 Sketch map to show the historical geography of the city of London-derry, 1609–1969

belonging to one O'Kane on the other side of the river, and, as he says, 'I daily sent workmen with a guard of soldiers to cut it down, and there was not a stick of it brought home but was first well fought for.'[9]

In 1606 Docwra left the town in the charge of Sir George Paulett, who neglected the fortifications. It was attacked on 19 April 1608 by Sir Cahir O'Doherty, and thus began the first of the three sieges which 'that ominous place'[10] was to endure in the seventeenth century. The garrison held out for two days, but was then overwhelmed; the upper and lower forts were taken and

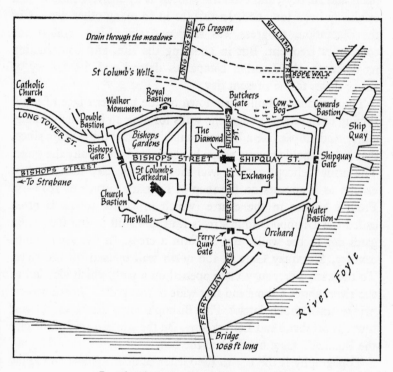

4 Londonderry in the eighteenth century

Paulett was killed. Shortly afterwards Sir Josias Bodley (younger brother of the founder of Bodleian library) reported that Derry had been 'wholly spoiled, ransacked and fired' and that at the time of the attack its fortifications had been 'much decayed and open to surprise'. In another report, some six months later, he recommended 'new gates and bridges to be made, the ditch digged deeper and broader in most places, houses of municon, victualles and other purposes to be made'.[11] The ramparts and parapets of the two forts were accordingly rebuilt, and cabins constructed for the returning population.

The site eventually chosen by the London companies for their new town of 'London-Derry' lay slightly to the north-east of Docwra's. The Londoners' obligation to enclose it with strong walls and fortifications was not fulfilled until 1619, after numerous plans and surveys, and even then not in as extensive a form as had originally been intended. In this, as in so many other aspects of the plantation, progress was slow and complaints against the companies frequent. But in choosing the site, and constructing its defences, the London companies determined the history of Derry down to the present day.

The Londoners built their town on the northern face of a hill sloping to the water's edge, the walls forming an irregular oblong, a distorted ellipse like a battered shield. All down the years since, that indescribable oblong shape has remained essentially the same. The army helicopter pilot who flies over the city today sees it exactly as it appears on the map of Pynnar's survey of 1618–19. From a square in the centre (which in Ulster towns is often called the Diamond) four streets lead downhill to the four main gates cut in the walls, and so form a cross. In the seventeenth century, Shipquay Gate in the north wall opened on the river. To the east, Ferryquay Gate opened on a path which also led to the river, about a thousand feet wide at this point. (There was no bridge until much later.) The Bishop's Gate faced south-west towards Strabane and Letterkenny. On the western side of the city the Butcher's Gate overlooked the bog.

Topography is the key to the Ulster conflict. Unless you know exactly who lives where, and why, much of it does not make sense. The difficulty outsiders experience in understanding Ulster's troubles arises from the fact that people who live there know this information to the square inch, while strangers know nothing of it. The topography of many small towns in Ulster has remained unchanged since the early seventeenth century at least. This simple fact may be equally true of many English villages, but it has not the same significance in England. There it does not determine the disposition of opposing forces in a battle which has never ended. For example, some Ulster towns, like Downpatrick and Dungannon, have an English Street, an Irish Street and a Scotch Street, which tell us of the original plantation disposition. Some Ulster villages have one main street with Catholics living at one end and Protestants at the other. To the foreigner who only reads about the Ulster problem in books, this might seem astonishing in itself, but far more interesting is the fact that the division was exactly the same in 1690. If you read old topographical guides to Belfast in the late eighteenth century you will find that 'Anderson's town' was even then a Catholic village outside a Presbyterian Belfast, and surrounded by a Presbyterian Co. Antrim. In Belfast itself you can still trace the exact point, near the city centre, where the Irish were allowed to settle by the town wall in the seventeenth century (see p. 62 below). In other cities new housing estates obliterate the singularities of past settlement, but in Belfast history shapes the character of the housing estates. In Derry this is even more obvious; topography is the key to almost every aspect of life.

The most obvious aspect of Derry's defences in the seventeenth century was not their strength but their weakness. This was apparent as soon as the walls were built, and became a source of unending complaint and recrimination. Not only were the walls inadequate for defence, as successive surveyors never tired of pointing out, but the whole town was tilted towards the river in such a way that ships had only to sail up to it and bombard it at will. On land it could be shelled in the same way from adjacent higher ground. The royal commission appointed by Charles I, as a result of the quarrel between the Crown and the city over whether the Londoners had fulfilled their covenants, found Derry 'so ill situated that both the walls, houses and streets lie open to the command of any shipping that shall come to the harbour, and also to divers hills about the town, and to many other inconveniences, so as in our judgment it is not a place of defence nor tenable if any foreign enemy should come before it.'[12]

The site was at one time an island, for the Foyle divided to the south of it, the main stream running on the east, and a smaller stream on the west, meandering through the 'bogg most commonlie wet'. This stream separated the town from the mainland, and was, as Docwra pointed out, not easily passable, except in two or three places. The problem of how to make it even less passable was to occupy military engineers for a long time to come. By the time of the great siege of 1689, the stream had dwindled to a mere burn, but at the spring tides water flooded in at either end and formed an excellent natural defence. The bog was used to pasture cattle, and is indicated on the early maps by the words 'bogg' or 'cow-bogg'. Raven's map of 1625 says 'Beast', a term still familiar in a region where the farmer calls his cattle 'the bastes'. Here in later times a cow market was established, and here today the Derry cattle markets are still situated.

On successive early seventeenth-century maps a pathway over the bog begins to sprout north-westward from the Butcher's Gate, like a questing antenna. By the eighteenth century it has become a road marked as 'the Bogside', and beyond it again is 'the Long Bogside' leading eventually to the village of Creggan. Before 1969 these little curiosities of topographical history were known only to those who lived there. In the last few years the Bogside and Creggan have become a part of the world's collective nightmare, just as once Nicosia's Ledra Street, 'Murder Mile', haunted the minds of television viewers in peaceful Ireland.

Thomas Raven's map of Londonderry, made in 1625, bears the title: 'A Plott of ye Cittie and [Is] land of Londonderry [with] a proiectment of [  ] outworkes, and the Cuttinge of the Bogg for the better securinge of ye Cittie.' The letterpress besides the outworks reads: 'The high Grownd lyennge nere without Bishopps Gate wch may be fortified with some outworkes of earth accordinge as the nature of the Grownd will best afford, either as here it is p' iected, or as may be thought most fyttinge, to hinder an Aproch to ye Towne wch yt Grownd doth naturally lye fitt for, if An Enemye of Power & policie be invader: These outworkes may the better be forborne if the bogg be cutt as aboue is expressed.' The line of the projected ditch through the bog bears the legend: 'The Dytch, here intended, to be Cutt 20 foot wide 10 foot Deepe. The Earth to be Cast inwardes wch will make a Rampier of good strength being made with some flankers.'[13]

The Bogside was always to be the weak point in the city's defences; it was the vulnerable western flank where unsubjugated

Ireland perpetually menaced the bastion of the plantation. There, outside the walls, the Catholic Irish were allowed to settle when only Protestants were allowed to dwell within the city. And whereas in Belfast the Irish were eventually permitted to enter the city because they were at first a tiny minority in a Protestant hinterland, in Derry they were kept out just because the city dwellers were a minority in a predominantly Catholic population. That is the peculiarity of the Derry situation, and the secret of its enduring siege. The London plantation was never, as it sometimes appears in Protestant mythology, a purely Protestant settlement which is slowly being overwhelmed by the Catholic population. It was more than half-Catholic from the very beginning, because the planters did not, and probably could not, keep the terms of their original undertaking. And Derry is indeed an island. The most curious aspect of all about its situation as an outwork of the plantation is that it lies on the wrong side of the river. The commission which inquired into the causes of the Londonderry riots in 1869 observed that 'the city and liberties are in Co. Donegal, where the Roman Catholics outnumber Protestants by three to one, yet Londonderry County is one of the most Protestant counties'.[14]

So the Bogside became Protestant Derry's bad dream, centuries before the August day in 1969 which flashed its name round the world. Once the essential pattern was established, not even the nineteenth-century expansion of the city over those water meadows and pleasant uplands could eradicate it. Beneath the maze of streets the subterranean fire eternally smouldered, because the course of Irish history never created the circumstances in which it could die out. The stretch of wall between the Butcher's Gate and the Bishop's Gate was the vital point in Derry's defences. Here at the projecting corner was built the great double bastion, and the Royal Bastion, from which was flown the crimson flag during the siege. Here in the early nineteenth century the Apprentice Boys erected the tall granite column of the Walker Monument to tower like a sentinel over the Bogside far below. It was blown to pieces in 1973 by an I.R.A. bomb. This was not the action of a modern guerrilla army striking at 'the occupation forces'; it belonged to a far older war.

# 3. The Crimson Flag

In 1642, after the rebellion, Derry became a city of refuge for the entire north of the plantation, and hundreds flocked to the safety of its walls. It was placed under the command of the Governor, Sir John Vaughan, who wrote to the lords justices in January 1642 that the entire county was 'a prey to the rebels, and all burnt to the river side, so that the enemy braves us at the ferry, and we dare not spend a shott at him for feare of wasting our little proporcion of powder, which wee keepe to defend the Walls when we shall be assaulted'. The refugees were menaced by starvation and disease, and vulnerable through their 'extreame want of armes'[15] (that phrase seems to run right through Ulster's history). The city was relieved by the prompt action of the London companies, who sent ships with food, clothing and all kinds of ammunition and arms, including ordnance. Some of these guns can be seen on the walls to this day. A pamphlet with the title *Newes from the North of Ireland* tells of a vast concourse of people who fled to Derry from the 'cruel murtherers and thirsty shedders of innocent blood', and asserts that if its walls had not received and sheltered them, not only the baronies of Raphoe and Innishowen, but all Ulster would have been lost.[16]

Once again we see the immense importance of the 1641 rebellion. It was then that the pattern of behaviour was formed which was to influence the fate of Derry, and of the province, in 1689 and in so many crises since. A 'league of captains' was formed to guard the walls, and they swore to be loyal to the King and State and to defend the city to the death. All the Catholic Irish were expelled from the city. Men were allocated to guard the ordnance and gates night and day, and the women and children were to stay indoors, and hang lights outside their houses at night. Activity of this kind is hardly distinguishable from what was going on in the streets of Londonderry in the 1970s.

In 1649 Derry was besieged once more, but this time by the

loyalist forces of Charles I under Lord Montgomery, while Sir Charles Coote with eight hundred foot and one hundred and eighty horse held the city for Parliament. The siege lasted twenty weeks until Coote made terms with the Irish leader Owen Roe O'Neill and, with his help, forced the besiegers to withdraw. It was a reversal of the 'normal' Derry siege situation, a bizarre consequence of the Civil War and Charles I's odd Irish alliances, and significantly it has not entered at all into the mythology of either Catholic or Protestant. Yet the siege was historically important, and, as far as the technical aspects of ordnance and fortification were concerned, it was a dress rehearsal for 1689. Confusion had overtaken all the conventional alignments. This time the loyalists were the besiegers, and the Presbyterians were outside the walls, while the Catholic Irish made alliance with the defenders, and for the moment were on the winning side.

The natural balance, in religion if not in loyalty, was restored with the great siege of 1689, which was to become the epic of the Protestant plantation and provide its enduring watchword, 'No Surrender'. Broadly, the siege of 1689 has two distinct kinds of historical significance. Each is valid in itself, but where they overlap some contradictions are apparent. The strange process whereby actual events are transmuted into folk-memory, a process which begins while the events are taking place, has inevitably expunged the contradictions, leaving a simpler and more dramatic version which is nevertheless in many ways more interesting. On one level, we may regard the siege of Derry as an important episode in the history of Ireland, of the British Isles and of western Europe; as a turning point in the struggle between William III and James II or Louis XIV. In any of these contexts we are aware that it is not merely of Irish significance. On another level, it may be examined as an episode, and a most significant one, in the long struggle between Catholic and Protestant for dominance in Ireland.

If we look at the siege as it really happened, and not as it has come to appear in Protestant legend, we at once become aware that it was never intended to be an episode in the Catholic–Protestant struggle at all. The reality was different from the legend in many ways, and we might even begin by considering whether any siege actually took place. Some Jacobite writers, notably Hilaire Belloc

and Sir George Petrie, have argued (partly as a corrective to
Macaulay) that the military operations around Derry did not
amount to a proper siege at all; at most they constituted a light

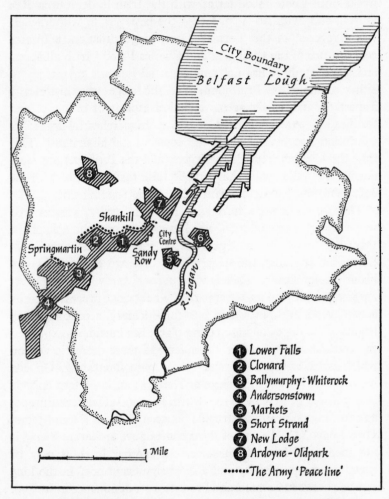

5 Areas of predominantly Catholic population in Belfast

siege and blockade combined.[17] This kind of Catholic sabotage
rouses the indignation of latter-day defenders of Derry's walls, who
can justly point out that there was nothing imaginary about the
sufferings of the besieged. Nevertheless it contains an element of

truth. The investment of Derry was very reluctantly undertaken, and once begun was conducted for a long time with a conspicuous lack of skill and enthusiasm. The defenders were allowed a long time to organize themselves, and the besiegers bent over backwards to give them every chance to reverse their decision, to such an extent that in reading accounts of the siege one cannot sometimes escape the feeling that it was imposed upon the royal forces by the defenders. When it became a matter of honour to James's commanders to take the city, they put their reliance on the blockade of the Foyle starving the defenders into surrender, rather than determined bloody attempts at storming the gates.

Obviously the siege was not intended to be a confrontation between Catholic and Protestant—it took that colour from events over which James II had no control, and which indeed had happened long before his birth. There were Protestants in the army which besieged Derry, and the attempt to take the city did not represent a Catholic threat to the Protestant religion. The loyalists were all on King James's side, and in theory what the defenders were doing was conducting a rebellion against their lawful sovereign, and proclaiming the cause of a usurper, William of Orange. The siege of Derry was only one episode in a war which James was fighting in Ireland to recover his throne. It is clear that there was no shadow of doubt about James's authority. Quite apart from his royal claims in England, he was in constitutional theory the legitimate King of Ireland. In resisting him, the defenders of Derry made a completely positive act of rebellion with full acceptance of the possible consequences. This was precisely why they were at first so divided on their course of action, and why Bishop Hopkins, and later Governor Lundy, left the city.

Moreover, in his operations against Derry, James showed himself cautious, intelligent and above all humane. The defenders, and those who venerate their memory, accredit him with the reverse of these attributes, but the evidence is not in doubt. What irritated James's officers was his moodiness and irresolution, his refusal to take firm and decisive action when it was needed. He insisted, at considerable risk and inconvenience, on seeing the walls for himself, and was shot at by the defenders, whereupon he returned to Dublin and appeared to lose interest in Derry. He was markedly more humane than his commanders, as was shown most dramatically in his intervention to release those Protestants whom his Lithuanian General Rosen had driven as hostages to the city walls. He refused to conduct war in that way, and did not conceal his anger and contempt for Rosen's ferocity, which he described as that of an animal. Throughout the campaign he showed a scrupulous regard for the contemporary laws of war.

Strangest of all, perhaps, in Protestant eyes, he displayed little of the religious bigotry which was shown by the defenders, and notably by the Rev. George Walker, whose siege sermons contain much anti-Catholic ranting. This seems the more remarkable since James had lost his throne and his inheritance precisely because of his inflexible religious and political aims, but it is nevertheless true. There is in reality no inconsistency, for the real James was not the cardboard villain of Orange legend, but a complex human being. So too was William III, who did not have to like Irish Protestants in order to make use of them, especially when their holding on to Derry proved successful. The tardiness of his sending aid to the city almost sealed their fate.

Finally, it is easy for Irishmen to overlook the fact that James II was an English Catholic, and, like many of his English co-religionists then and since, had little empathy with Irish Catholics. They wanted ultimately to achieve aims which were not his and were indeed often inimical to his basic strategy. Their primary concern was to reverse the Restoration land settlement and regain the estates taken from them by Cromwell. For James, Ireland and the Irish were only a means to an end, the recovery of his kingdom, but he did not want to regain England at the cost of giving Ireland greater independence.

The 'Irish' significance of the siege stemmed from an incident which took place far away from Derry's walls. On Monday 3 December 1688 an anonymous letter was found on the streets of Comber, a village in Co. Down. It was addressed to a Protestant nobleman, Lord Mount-Alexander, and it read:

Good my Lord,
   I have written to let you know that all our Irishmen through Ireland is sworn: that on the ninth day of this month they are all

to fall on to kill and murder man, wife and child; and I desire
your lordship to take care of yourself, and all others that are
judged by our men to be heads, for whosoever of them can kill
any of you, they are to have a captain's place; so my desire to
your honour is, to look to yourself, and give other noblemen
warning, and go not out either night or day without a good
guard with you, and let no Irishman come near you, whatsoever
he be; so this is all from him who was your father's friend, and
is your friend, and will be, though I dare not be known, as yet,
for fear of my life.[18]

Copies of the 'Comber letter' were quickly distributed all over
Ulster. It was not the start of the panic among Protestants, which
had really begun as soon as James's policy in Ireland had become
clear to them, but the warning came just at the right moment
to have the maximum effect on the Protestant mind. In other words,
it was probably created by the fears which it stimulated. Un-
questionably, it was a 'vile hoax', a cleverly timed piece of propaganda, yet few Protestants doubted its authenticity, for it spoke
in the ancestral voice. It reached Derry on Friday, 7 December,
and very probably, as Witherow claims, 'it resulted in the siege
of Derry and lost James Ireland'.[19] The Presbyterians after all
had some cause to welcome James's policy of toleration for non-
conformists after the stern Anglican repression of Charles's reign.
It was intended to relieve the Catholics, but they might also have
benefited from it, and they might very well have taken James's
side, or at least not resisted him. The siege was incidentally the
archetypal situation in which the Presbyterians sank their differences with the Established Church in order to defend Protestantism.
In *The Montgomery Manuscripts* we read that the Protestants of
Ulster confederated for their safety against such a massacre as that
of 1641. At this time the Presbyterians required no renewal of their
covenant, but joined with the clergy of the Church of Ireland
against the common enemy. 'Then they scrupled not (nor wee)
to hear one another's way of worship and sermons.'[20]

In popular legend, the events of the siege have long since
crystallized into a series of episodes like the 'Comber letter', each
of which has enormous symbolical significance. Worn smooth by

time and usage, they still serve a useful purpose in the unending war and tell us much about the nature of that war. The Comber letter led to the shutting of the gates, for it reached the city at the same time as MacDonnell's regiment. The Redshanks, who were little more than an armed mob, were inevitably regarded as the agents of the planned massacre. The citizens of Derry were thus placed in a dilemma. They could not seek the advice and help of the government in time, so they had to make a decision on the spot, and it was the young and hot-headed who decided for their elders.

The motive for shutting the gates was not to declare loyalty to William, but to secure the Protestants and to keep Catholics out of the city. In the words of one historian of the siege, 'It was not an unbridled enthusiasm for the cause of the Prince of Orange that led the inhabitants to refuse admission to King James's troops. The real motive underlying that act of rebellion was the instinct of self-preservation.'[21]

The memory of the thirteen apprentices who seized the keys and shut the gates is perpetuated in the brotherhood of the Apprentice Boys of Derry, with seven parent clubs within the walls, and branches throughout Ulster, and in England, Scotland and America. Only those initiated within the walls are permitted to be full members. In 1826 they erected an eighty-one-foot-high pillar, surmounted by a statue of the Rev. George Walker, who was Governor during the siege, at a point on the walls overlooking the Bogside. Nearby, within the walls, stands the Apprentice Boys' Hall, built in 1873. Their emblem is the crimson flag or badge, commemorating Colonel Michelburn's 'bloody flag', the flag of defiance which flew from the Royal Bastion and from the Cathedral in 1689,

> *That crimson flag which on the steeple flies*
> *Tells Rosen that his forces it defies. . . .*[22]

'It was at noon that the gates were shut,' writes Witherow, 'and soon after Bishop Hopkins came down to the Diamond, and made a speech to the multitude, and warned them of the dangerous consequences which would ensue.'[23] An essential part of the ritual which always takes place when the plantation shuts the gates is that there must be a Bishop Hopkins to point out the danger of defying the lawful supreme authority, even in the interests of self-preservation, and ultimately the decision must be made on instinct and not on logic, however sound. It may well be that instinct is a dangerous guide, and that men should always be led by reason, but this does not seem to be how the world works, nor is it the nature of man. History shows that the instinct to resist, against overwhelming odds, is often justified in the event.

The shutting of the gates is a ritual which is repeated over and over again in the history of the plantation. For example, in 1912, when Bonar Law, leader of the Conservative Party, pledged Conservative support for the Ulster Protestants' resistance to the third Home Rule Bill, he told the Ulster Volunteer Force, 'Once again you hold the pass, the pass for the Empire. You are a besieged city. The timid have left you; your Lundys have betrayed you; but you have closed your gates.'[24]

Behind the heroic decisiveness of the action many doubts were concealed. Some men chose to avoid the confrontation, others to resist to the last. This is the permanent duality of the Protestant defence: it has persisted since, and it ran through the most recent crisis. When the decision is made, a scapegoat must be found for all the misgivings that had earlier been expressed. Lieutenant-Colonel Lundy, a Scottish episcopalian from Dunbarton, became military governor of Derry as the result of an agreement between the revolted citizens and James's Protestant General, Lord Mountjoy. Lundy was a good soldier, a cautious, loyal and prudent man who was unhappy at the city's change of allegiance. He was, writes J. G. Simms, 'not a traitor but a defeatist'.[25] He nevertheless became the scapegoat for all the doubts of the defenders. When he slipped out of the city in disguise, and with a load of match tied to his back, he carried away with him the burden of the city's anxiety and irresolution. The annual burning of the effigy of Lundy by the Apprentice Boys is not, therefore, a meaningless and barbarous custom, but an act of ritual purgation. When the Apprentice Boys fire the toy cannon, set fire to the matches, and hoist the effigy on the walls, they are resolving the crisis of conscience. They have made up their minds again: the cry is to be 'No Surrender'.

Other episodes of the siege have come to fulfil the same kind of purpose. In June 1689, after several attempts to offer terms to the garrison, Lieutenant-General Hamilton drew up formal proposals for surrender, and had them sent into the city inside a dead shell, which is to this day preserved in Derry Cathedral. The defenders were by this time close to starvation, and were existing, according to Walker's account, on horse flesh, dogs, cats, rats and mice, salted hides, tallow and starch.[26] But they refused Hamilton's terms, saying that they wondered that he should expect them to trust the sincerity of one who had once before broken faith with King William III. (In January 1689 Hamilton was released from the Tower of London to treat with the Earl of Tyrconnell, who was believed to be about to transfer his allegiance to the Prince of Orange. Once in Dublin, however, Hamilton put himself at Tyrconnell's disposal.)

The episode of the dead shell led directly to the only really determined assault on the walls. The young Donough Macarthy, Lord Clancarty, had lately joined the Jacobite army with his regiment from Munster. There was, so it was said, an old prophecy that a Clancarty should one day knock at the gates of Derry. Accordingly at about ten o'clock on the night of 28 June, Clancarty at the head of his regiment had come over the Bogside and attacked the Butcher's Gate. The few defenders who were in the trenches were taken by surprise and rapidly retreated before a salvo of grenades. The besiegers took the outworks, and their miners entered a cellar underneath the Gunner's Bastion. While this was going on, a detachment of defenders filed out of the Bishop's Gate and crept along the wall, holding their fire until they had almost reached the enemy. Then, in Walker's words, they 'thundred upon them'[27] while case-shot and small-shot were poured down from the walls. Clancarty's men were repulsed from the outworks, and fell back in confusion across the bog, leaving behind thirty dead and the miners. The prediction was fulfilled, said the Protestants: Clancarty had knocked at the gates, but he did not get in.

A few days later, General Rosen rounded up all the Protestants within ten miles' radius of the city, whether they had protections from the Jacobites or not, and drove them under the walls, the action which James so swiftly and so angrily condemned. His motive was to force the defenders to take them in, since he knew they could not both feed them and continue the siege for more than a few days. At first the refugees were mistaken for the enemy and fired upon from the walls. 'We were troubled when we found the mistake,' writes Walker, 'but it supported us to a great degree, when we found that none of them were touch'd by our Shot, which by the direction of Providence (as if every Bullet had its Commission what to do) spared them, and found out and kill'd three of the Enemy.'[28] The garrison's grim reply to Rosen's threat was to erect a gallows on the walls and offer to hang the prisoners they held if the distressed people were not permitted to return to their homes. Rosen relented on 4 July, and the defenders took advantage of the incident by surreptitiously augmenting the numbers of the refugees with several hundred of their starving and useless people, and by recruiting a few able-bodied men for the defence. The gallows was dismantled, and the prisoners were spared.

The miseries of the starving garrison were not lessened by the fact that throughout June and July the masts of the English ships could be seen in the distance on Lough Foyle. Why the attempt to relieve the city was not made six weeks earlier is something of a mystery. Kirk, the English commander, did not act until he had explicit orders to help the garrison, and when finally he began to move up the Foyle, the risk to his ships had greatly increased.

On 28 July two merchant ships, the *Mountjoy*, commanded by Micaiah Browning, a native of Londonderry, and the *Phoenix*, sailed up the Foyle towards the boom, escorted by the thirty-six-gun frigate *Dartmouth*. The river was low, and the only navigable channel ran close to the left bank, where the Jacobite batteries were situated. While the *Dartmouth* engaged the batteries, the *Mountjoy* sailed on to the boom. It cracked and broke, but the *Mountjoy* rebounded and ran aground. Yelling in triumph, the Jacobite soldiers swarmed down the banks to board her, but were driven back by the *Dartmouth*'s guns, and the ship was refloated. The *Phoenix* had already passsed through the shattered boom, and at nightfall the three ships tied up at Derry quay, and unloaded for the famished city six thousand bushels of meal, 'cheeses, casks of beef, flitches of bacon, kegs of butter, sacks of pease and biscuit, ankers of brandy'.

'The bonfires shone bright along the whole circuit of the ramparts,' Macaulay tells us. 'The Irish guns continued to roar all night; and all night the bells of the rescued city made answer to the Irish guns with a peal of joyous defiance.' For three days more the bombardment continued, but on the third night flames were seen rising from the Jacobite camp, and on the morning of 1 August the citizens saw in the distance 'the long column of pikes and standards retreating up the left bank of the Foyle towards Strabane'.[29]

Those bonfires still blaze in the streets of Belfast and Derry. They are among the most enduring signals used by either community to indicate a victory over the other. The red leaping flames, lighting up the wild and passionate intensity of gaunt Ulster faces, are a well-remembered element in every Ulster childhood, even the most sheltered. It may be despised, condemned, arouse revulsion and even horror—a spectacle so primitive that outsiders find it incomprehensible—but to an Ulsterman it speaks unmistakably of home. Like so much in the pattern of Ulster behaviour, it makes no sense without the code. It means so much more than it appears to mean.

# 4. At the Butcher's Gate

It is noteworthy that Macaulay, as an English Whig, ends his epic account of the siege with some mild strictures of the manner of its commemoration. Remarking that the anniversaries of the day on which the gates were closed and of the day on which the siege was raised were still celebrated by salutes, processions, banquets and sermons, he concedes that such sentiment 'belongs to the higher and purer part of human nature, which adds not a little to the strength of states', but continues: 'Yet it is impossible for the moralist or the statesman to look with unmixed complacency on the solemnities with which Londonderry commemorates her deliverance, and on the honours which she pays to those who saved her. Unhappily the animosities of her brave champions have descended with their glory. The faults which are ordinarily found in dominant castes and dominant sects have not seldom shown themselves without disguise at her festivities; and even with the expressions of pious gratitude which have resounded from her pulpits have too often been mingled words of wrath and defiance.'[30]

Here, in a nutshell, is the argument which has gone on ever since. The Commission of Inquiry on the Londonderry riots of 1869 made the same point, that it was in its 'double aspect' that the celebration became a cause of anger and offence. Few states committed the imprudence of continuing to celebrate a victory in a civil war: in ancient times both the Greeks and the Romans had been careful never to tolerate it.[31]

The formal celebration of the siege did not begin, however, until the late eighteenth century. The centenary coincided with a time of unusual self-confidence for the 'Protestant nation' which effectively ruled Ireland. The apogee of Protestant nationalism was expressed in the Volunteer movement during the 1780s. Safer than it had ever been before in Ireland from the threat of a Catholic *revanche*, the Ascendancy devoted its main political activity to winning concessions from the supreme government in London, and in asserting Ireland's independence. An early nineteenth-century history of the siege by the Rev. John Graham contains an interesting account of the centenary commemoration in 1788, which enables us to see how the celebration of the historic event might have developed in a more 'natural' way, allowing the townsfolk of both creeds to take civic pride in it.

He tells us that the dawn of 7 December 1788 was announced by the beating of drums, the ringing of bells and the firing of the cannon used in the siege. The crimson flag flew from the Cathedral. The mayor and corporation, the clergy, officers of the Royal Navy, the 46th Regiment and the Volunteer corps went in procession from the Ship Quay to the Cathedral, where the Dean preached a sermon, and the oratorio *Judas Maccabeus* was performed, with the air ''Tis Liberty, dear Liberty alone'. For the Presbyterians, the Rev. Mr. Black gave an oration at the meeting house. H.M.S. *Porcupine* entered the harbour, dressed overall, on purpose to honour the festival, and the guns on the ramparts replied to her salute.

While this was going on 'some of the lower class of citizens' appeared with an effigy representing 'the well-known Lundy, executed in a very humorous style, with a bundle of matches on its back'. With this they perambulated the streets, and 'having repeatedly exposed it to the insults of the zealous populace, they burned it in the market place with every circumstance of ignominy'. At two o'clock the Apprentice Boys' Company went through the ceremonial of shutting the gates. They then returned to the Diamond with King James's colours in triumph, and a *feu-de-joie* was fired. At four o'clock 'the mayor and corporation, the clergy, the officers of the navy and army, the clergy of the Church of Rome, the gentlemen from the country, volunteers, citizens, scholars and apprentices set down to a plain but plentiful dinner in the Town Hall. Religious dissensions, in particular, seemed to be buried in oblivion, and Roman Catholics vied with Protestants in expressing, by every possible mark, their sense of the blessings secured to them by the event which they were commemorating.—'

Significantly, however, the author goes on to say that this cordiality stood on record 'in strong contrast with the brutal ignorance of the agitators of the present day, who load the name of their deliverer with obloquy and consider the honours paid to his memory as an insult to their religion'.[32] He is writing in 1829, at the climax of the campaign for Catholic emancipation, and though his tendentious reference to the O'Connellites is only one side of the argument, it reveals that Catholics already regarded any Williamite celebrations as 'an insult to their religion'.

This view gained ground after Catholic emancipation when Orangeism became increasingly unpopular in the eyes of English governments. In 1834 the English traveller Inglis was shown the trophies of the siege in the Cathedral by a Derry man who bitterly lamented that the good old days were gone by when Orangemen might show their colours. 'The 12th of August', he said, 'had passed away with only the firing of a few guns—these were poor doings for Derry.'[33]

The nonsectarian celebration of the siege was therefore of very short duration, and did not survive the climate of 1798 and the

Union. Almost certainly the relaxed atmosphere of the centenary year owed something to the afterglow of the Volunteer era, and to the influence of the benignly pro-Catholic Bishop of Derry and Earl of Bristol, Frederick Augustus Hervey. With the founding of the Apprentice Boys' society in 1823 the relief celebrations resumed the more familiar divisive form, although they do not appear to have caused serious communal clashes in the first half of the century. After 1860, however, animosity became more acute. The agent of change was a technological advance which at first sight would seem to have little to do with sectarian strife—the invention of railways.

The most austere of the Ulster Protestants did not greet the arrival of the locomotive in the 1840s and 1850s with much enthusiasm, since it increased the mobility of sinfulness, especially on the Sabbath. 'Every sound of the railway whistle', thundered one Presbyterian minister, 'is answered by a shout in hell',[34] (a local variation of the *mot* of the similarly minded Pope Leo XIII, '*Chemins de fer, chemins d'enfer*'). The introduction of the excursion train proved a boon to the resurgent Orange Order, however, and enabled thousands of Orangemen from outlying areas, and from the entire province, to pour into Derry on 12 August for the annual celebration, as they still do to this day.

Though they might in all sincerity protest that they were not interfering with local Catholics, the Orangemen by these incursions created a perfect example of the disturbance of the territorial equilibrium. It was one thing for local Apprentice Boys to hold their strange rites under the mocking but tolerant eyes of Catholic neighbours—as Derrymen they would banter each other about it next day—but it was a different matter for them to be supported by large numbers of strangers, no doubt with vastly increased potential for provocation, implied or direct, making the message clear that Catholics were to be kept in their place, which was emphatically outside the walls.

This challenge, and the counter-challenge provided by the Fenian ferment of the 1860s, provoked a series of fierce riots in the city. In July 1868, after trouble about processions, some Apprentice Boys fired salvoes of broken crockery over the Bogside from the Walker Monument. In the following December a Catholic procession invaded the Protestant Waterside district with a band playing 'the Wearing of the Green'. Shots were fired at them. In February 1869 Catholic processions forced their way through police cordons at the Butcher's Gate and the Bishop's Gate, while missiles flew 'like a shower of hailstones'. The most serious riot occurred on 28 April 1869, following the arrival in the city of His Royal Highness Prince Arthur. The prince was met by a Catholic procession and a Protestant one. Both bands played 'God Save the Queen', but then played 'their own peculiar airs' to their mutual annoyance. In the evening Catholic crowds, shouting for 'an Irish Republic' and carrying green flags, surged through the Diamond. Rioting and shooting broke out; the Catholics were trapped within the walls by Protestant rioters, and indignantly complained to the police that their traditional line of retreat back through the Butcher's Gate to the Bogside had been treacherously blocked—there could be no clearer example of the highly ritual character of such encounters. Three men were killed, and scores injured, and a commission of inquiry was appointed to discover the causes of the riot.

'Sad as the results were,' the commissioners reported, 'we can only express our surprise that they were not worse. The constabulary fired a volley in a crowded street; conflicting mobs not only assailed each other violently with stones, but revolvers were freely used by each body against the other. . . . Surely it is a matter for rejoicing that a riot of such a character caused the loss of only three human lives.'[35] The story was to be repeated in 1883, when the proximate cause of the riots was a visit by the nationalist Lord Mayor of Dublin to deliver a speech on 'Franchise'. In vain the police tried to avoid trouble by diverting the mayor's procession away from the eastern portions of the city and in the direction of the Bogside, where 'the headquarters of the Nationalist party and the rooms of the Nationalist League' were situated. The Apprentice Boys had intended to stage a protest meeting on a platform at the Walker Monument. Instead they formed a procession, and, headed by a band, 'set off, with their usual crimson flag and Union Jacks flying' down to the Diamond, where they seized the town hall, and from it fired upon the Catholic procession as it approached. The

Catholics returned the fire, and then there followed slates, stones and missiles. By nightfall there was serious rioting outside the Bishop's Gate. Subsequently another commission of inquiry sat, marvelling that 'only two persons received wounds of a serious character'.[36]

Thus neither the location nor the character of the rioting which on 12 August 1969 led to the 'Battle of the Bogside' was coincidental. The chosen field of the encounter and the formal rules of combat were determined at a time long distant. The open ground beyond the wall from the Bishop's Gate to the Butcher's Gate is a volcanic zone where the hurling of a brick or the firing of a pistol can start an earthquake.

# PART THREE

# The Politics of Presbytery

# 1. Old Darkness

If the distinction between planter and Gael in the Ulster of the seventeenth century cannot be satisfactorily explained in terms of race or culture (in the widest sense), it is more clearly comprehensible in terms of religion. Examination of the plantation poses the question: why were the Scots and English planters the only invaders not to assimilate in time with the indigenous population? The obvious answer is that they were the first to come after the Reformation. Their religion was the barrier which cut them off from the native Irish and placed them permanently in a state of siege. The gulf fixed between planter and Gael was the wider in that it resulted from the confrontation of extremes, of the Roman Church with the Calvinism of the Scottish lowlanders. One must be careful about categorizing the early Scots settlers, for they were not all Calvinists, and some indeed were Catholic, but in the main they represented Calvinist doctrine in its most uncompromising form, and here again the determinant factor is less the original planters than the sustaining flow of Calvinists into north-eastern Ireland for more than a century afterwards.

To understand the nature of the quarrel we must go back to the preceding century. It was in the sixteenth century, and not in the seventeenth, that the die was cast. The intensity of the emotions aroused by the Anglo-Irish dispute stems from one simple historical fact—that the Reformation was imposed on Britain at a time when the royal authority could not be exerted over all, or even very much, of Ireland. It was a time when the Tudors ruled Ireland more by alliance with the chieftains than by force. Given the choice between subduing the Irish and leaving them quietly in the exercise of their religion, English statesmen chose the latter course. As always with Ireland, they took the easy way, and hoped for better opportunities of strengthening the Reformation Church later. The opportunities never came, and the fact that the vast bulk of the Irish population remained Catholic is a reflection of the military, economic and administrative failure of Tudor sovereigns to exert their will over Ireland in the secular sphere. Had the British Isles as a whole remained Catholic, or had the Reformed religion been adopted in Ireland, a mild movement for independence would probably have developed in Ireland during the nineteenth century. It would undoubtedly have been successful without much bloodshed in the twentieth, and some form of devolved government, like that adopted for Northern Ireland after 1920, might have been the intermediate stage. But what gave the enduring Anglo-Irish conflict its peculiar bitterness was the difference in religion between the two islands and, even more, its political and strategic implications. By remaining Catholic, Ireland became the Achilles' heel of an England at war with the Catholic powers of Europe. Spain in the sixteenth century, and France in the eighteenth, saw the Irish as allies and Ireland as a foothold for the invasion of the British Isles as a whole. Thus the opponents of Catholic emancipation in the eighteenth century were not motivated so much by religious bigotry as by understandable fears that a Catholic-dominated parliament might side with the enemies of Hanoverian England, while even supporters, such as Edmund Burke, stressed that Catholic representation in an unreformed parliament would be minimal. Such strategic considerations have persisted almost to the present, and they help to explain why the Union was maintained long after Britain had conceded the independence of Ireland in principle, and why politico-religious rancour survived in Ireland when it had disappeared elsewhere.

By the time of the Ulster plantation, therefore, the dispossessing of Irish proprietors, and the planting of Protestant colonists, was a quite deliberate effort to strengthen the Protestant and British element in Ireland. James and his advisers had no reason to disguise this motive. The creation of new boroughs, for example, was explicitly to overcome the power of the Catholic recusants in the Irish parliament. These recusants were for the most part Old English, themselves planters in origin, and the element through which English authority in Ireland had operated in earlier times. The reign of James saw the first struggle between them and the new planters, a struggle which would eventually lead to the Old

English becoming completely identified with the Irish, and becoming indeed the natural leaders of the first coherent movement of Catholic nationalism in Ireland.

The character and motives of the new settlers may not have been all that their descendants would wish for in Ulster's founding fathers. The description of them given by the Rev. Andrew Stewart, minister of Donaghadee from 1645 to 1671, is often quoted, and rarely without malice.

'. . . And from Scotland came many, and from England not a few, yet all of them generally the scum of both nations, who, for debt, or breaking and fleeing from justice, or seeking shelter, came hither, hoping to be without fear of man's justice in a land where there was nothing, or but little, as yet, of the fear of God. And in a few years there flocked such a multitude of people from Scotland that these northern counties of Down, Antrim, Londonderry, &c., were in a good measure planted, which had been waste before. . . .

'And verily at this time the whole body of this people seemed ripe, and soon ripe for the manifestation, in a greater degree, of God's judgments or mercy than had been seen for a long time; for their carriage made them to be abhorred at home in their native land, insomuch that going for Ireland was looked on as a miserable mark of a deplorable person—yea, it was turned into a proverb, and one of the worst expressions of disdain that could be invented was to tell a man that Ireland would be his hinder end.'[1]

His account is corroborated by that of another minister, Robert Blair. 'Although amongst those whom Divine Providence did send to Ireland, there were several persons eminent for birth, education and parts; yet the most part were such as either poverty, scandalous lives, or, at the best, adventurous seeking of better accommodation had forced thither, so that the security and thriving of religion was little seen to by those adventurers, and the preachers were generally of the same complexion with the people.' Blair indeed had to wrestle with his own repugnance before he resigned himself to God's will. 'When I landed in Ireland, some men parting from their cups, and all things smelling of a root called rampions [wild garlic], my prejudice was confirmed against that land. But next day travelling towards Bangor, I met unexpectedly with so sweet a peace and so great a joy, as I behoved to look thereon as my welcome thither; and retiring to a private place about a mile above Craigfergus, I prostrated myself upon the grass to rejoice in the Lord, who proved the same to me in Ireland which He had been in Scotland. Nevertheless, my aversion to a settlement there continued long.'[2]

By any standard, this nucleus of Scottish Calvinist ministers included some remarkable men. Blair, brought to Bangor by Hamilton, had been a professor in Glasgow. Livingstone, who settled at Killinchy, was a great-grandson of Lord Livingstone, the guardian of Mary, Queen of Scots. We are told that 'he was skilled not only in Greek, Latin, Hebrew and Chaldaic, but had also knowledge of French, Italian, German, Spanish and Dutch'.[3] Cunningham, minister at Holywood, had been chaplain to the Earl of Buccleuch's regiment in Holland.

That these ministers should leave Scotland because of their opposition to prelacy, and immediately allow themselves to be ordained by Irish bishops, seems at first very puzzling. Why should a man like Robert Blair, for example, who resigned as regent in the College of Glasgow because he opposed the prelatic views of the new principal Dr. Cameron, quietly accept ordination from Bishop Echlin of Down? Blair says of his ordination, in Bangor on 10 July 1623, that Echlin declared, 'I know you account a presbytery to have divine warrant; will you not receive ordination from Mr Cunningham and the adjacent brethren, and let me come in among them in no other relation than a presbyter?' Their enemies might allege that this is characteristic hypocrisy, but it must be remembered that the position with regard to ordination in Scotland was still confused, and that this *modus vivendi* was made easier by the fact that Echlin of Down was himself a Scot, one of those designedly appointed by James, who wanted both to strengthen the Anglican Church and to advance his own country-men, particularly in Ulster.

It was a sensible mode of proceeding, but it created a situation which pleased neither the bishops nor the presbyters, and it ended with the rise of Laudian influence after 1633. The more open Presbyterians were ousted from their livings, forced to flee to Scotland and assume the not uncongenial stance of a minority persecuted for their religious belief. In 1636 this episcopal pressure caused a group of Presbyterians to build a ship, the *Eaglewing*, and set sail from Groomsport in Co. Down for New England with one hundred and forty emigrants, including the ministers Blair, Livingstone, Hamilton and McClelland. This imitation of the *Mayflower* was defeated by contrary winds, and after being buffeted off Newfoundland for two months, the emigrants returned home in distress to face the gibes of the episcopalians. The latter would reject the imputation that the Presbyterians were actually persecuted. For the Church of Ireland to enforce its doctrinal laws on its own clergy can hardly be described as persecution, and even the *Eaglewing* episode was more the consequence of complicated links with the Puritan colonists than of actual ill-usage, but the Presbyterian system was born in opposition, and its adherents have never been inclined to minimize the sacrifices made for principle.

The Presbyterian is happiest when he is being a radical. The austere doctrines of Calvinism, the simplicity of his worship, the democratic government of his Church, the memory of the martyred Covenanters, and the Scottish refusal to yield or to dissemble—all these incline him to that difficult and cantankerous disposition which is characteristic of a certain kind of political radicalism. His natural instinct is to distrust the outward forms of civil government unless they are consonant with his religious principles. On the other hand, his situation and his history in a predominantly Catholic Ireland have bred in him attitudes which seem opposite to these, making him defensive, intolerant and uncritically loyal to traditions and institutions. His special kind of political outlook has been accurately defined as 'settler radicalism'.[4]

The anomalies and paradoxes embraced by this settler radicalism are complex and little understood either by southern Irishmen or by the British ministers who have from time to time been called upon to deal with the Ulster problem. They have been more apparent at certain times in the past than at others, and at one period, between 1791 and 1798, they had a determinant influence on the course of Irish history, when they gave birth to the United Irish movement. In the twentieth century, when the Presbyterians seem to be the major element of the Protestant hegemony in Northern Ireland, it is easy to forget that the radical and anti-establishment aspects of Presbyterian politics are never far beneath the surface. Cabinet ministers may not even be aware of how easily political direction or pressure from the government can come to seem in Presbyterian eyes like persecution for principle's sake. The dissenter has sound historical reasons for being sensitive on this point, and it is hardly possible to exaggerate the deep sense of pride which he can take in the realization that he may be called upon to emulate his covenanting forbears in resisting the tyranny of overweening and unjust governments. It comes close to the Catholic pride which identifies Irish nationhood with the cause of a persecuted and outlawed religion.

The renewal of the National Covenant in Scotland in 1638, and the consequent commotions, had an immediate and direct effect in Ulster. The close connection with the mother church was shown by the fact that all four of the ministers who had sailed in the *Eaglewing* were members of the assembly which in Scotland, after the signing of the Covenant, abolished innovations in worship, deposed the bishops and re-established the Presbyterian system. Once more the Scots of Antrim and Down became an object of great suspicion to the government. This was a reversion to a pattern broken only by James I's accession, and which was to continue uninterrupted to the end of the eighteenth century, and in a rather different form ever since.

Thomas Wentworth, Archbishop Laud's friend and ally, was Lord Deputy in Ireland from 1633 to 1640. He acted resolutely to neutralize the Ulster Presbyterians' support for the Scottish resistance. By the 'Black Oath' of 1639, everyone in Ulster over sixteen was required to swear on the Gospels that he renounced the Covenant. At the same time efforts were made to cut off all correspondence with Scotland and to raise an army in Ulster, either to invade Scotland on the west or to keep the Ulster Covenanters quiet. This kind of treatment simply makes the Presbyterian more stubborn; he regards it as good for moulding character, and it was in these times that the mentality of resistance was formed which was to be displayed in Ulster in 1912–14 and in 1974. Many accepted the yoke of outward conformity in dour rebellious silence, and others who openly resisted were forced into exile. 'They were fined and imprisoned,' writes one Presbyterian historian, 'they left the homes they had builded, and the fields made fertile by their sweat and toil, and fled to Scotland'.[5] Incredible as it now seems, hundreds of ordinary people who had been deprived of their ministers rowed across the North Channel to Scotland on Sunday afternoons to take communion, and returned the same day. Livingstone records that on one occasion 'over 500 persons from Co. Down crossed the sea to receive the sacrament at Stranraer'.[6]

It is possible that if James I and his son had not tried so hard to impose conformity of organization and practice in religion throughout their kingdoms, less religious intolerance would have developed in Scotland and Ireland. Charles, much more than his father, was incapable of comprehending the nature of Presbyterian piety. Again and again this situation was to be re-created, right up to the present. Those in authority were simply unable to comprehend the dissenters' mentality, and so dismissed their objections as superficial or, worse, hypocritical. But to the Presbyterians, spiritual attitudes were paramount, and above all, rightly or wrongly, their own conception of freedom of worship and the claims of the state. They fully expected, and accepted, persecution for their beliefs. As the Galloway minister, Samuel Rutherford, declared in 1631, 'I desire not to go on the lee-side or sunny side of religion, or to put truth betwixt me and a storm: my Saviour did not so for me, who in His sufferings took the windy side of the hill.'[7]

## 2. Watchmen in Sion

In some ways Presbyterians suffered less than other Protestants from the effects of the 1641 rebellion. In the early stages of the rising only the English planters were attacked and the Scots were left alone, and although this immunity did not last long, it gave thousands of the Scots time to seek refuge and prepare defences. Even the Wentworth persecution now proved a blessing in disguise, for many of the Presbyterian ministers owed their lives to the fact that they were in exile in Scotland, and these men were able to return after 1642 and help to reorganize their church. They benefited, too, from the fact that the episcopal church in Ulster had virtually been swept away by the rebellion, and the Presbyterian system was thus able to expand greatly at its expense. These trends were encouraged by the extraordinary course of events in England after 1642, which forced first Parliament and then the King into alliance with the Scottish Presbyterians.

In April 1642 General Monro landed in Ireland with a Scottish army of some four thousand to help suppress the rebellion. The chaplains of this force, being ordained ministers of the Church of Scotland, at once began the task of reconstructing a Presbyterian church organization, and after creating four kirk sessions in the army, they formed a presbytery which met at Carrickfergus on Friday 10 July 1642. This presbytery remained the chief court of the church until 1654, when new presbyteries had to be formed because of the spread of congregations beyond Antrim and Down. In 1654 presbyteries were created for Antrim, Down and Route (the area about Ballymoney in North Antrim); in 1657 the presbytery of Laggan was formed out of Route (for the St. Johnstown area of Donegal) and in 1659 the presbytery of Tyrone was formed out of Down. These presbyteries met in synod, as circumstances required, until 1661, when the Synod was suppressed by the Restoration government.

The renaissance of 1642 was soon to be overshadowed by political and military events. Monro's army had been built up to a force of ten thousand, and, by its early success against the Irish rebels, had given confidence and political importance to the Scots settlers. But on 5 June 1646 the Ulster Irish under Owen Roe O'Neill inflicted a crushing defeat on Monro at Benburb. Over three thousand of his men were slain, against some seventy Irish: Sir Hugh Montgomery, the Lord of Ards, was taken prisoner with twenty-one other officers; and the entire Scots army was routed, leaving on the battlefield their artillery, arms, provisions, tents and baggage, along with thirty-two of their colours. So overwhelming a defeat produced consternation among the settlers, and many fled again into Scotland. The situation was desperate, for the counties of Antrim and Down lay open to O'Neill. Monro, fleeing to Lisburn without his wig and coat, sent for assistance to the Laggan Force, a body raised among the Donegal Presbyterians, and called on the country to rise and on every household to provide volunteers. The remnants of his army were regrouped to hold the borders of the Scottish settlements.

Not for the last time, the Ulster Scots were saved by political developments in the south of Ireland. O'Neill failed to follow up his victory, and turned instead to support his ally, the papal nuncio Rinuccini, in overthrowing the supreme council of the Confederates of Kilkenny. The Presbyterians characteristically saw Benburb as a punishment for their sins, the stroke of the righteous hand of God 'especially upon the Scotch army'. Monro was called 'a guilty proud party'. Many of his soldiers, wrote Adair, 'were prodigiously profane and wicked in their lives, and set themselves to prey upon the poor country scarce crept from under the ashes of a horrid rebellion'. Monro himself expressed the same opinion, but more tersely. 'For aught I can understand the Lord of Hosts had a controversy with us.'[8]

The complicated twists and turns of the 'war of the three kingdoms' were to impose strange vicissitudes on the Ulster Scots. The bitter rift between the Scottish Church and the Scottish Parliament over the Engagement (the secret treaty which the imprisoned Charles made with the Scottish commissioners) extended its baleful effects to Ulster; and the commander of the Parliamentary forces, General George Monck, was able to take advantage of the divisions among the Presbyterians to secure for Parliament the garrison towns of Belfast, Carrickfergus and Londonderry, the circumstance which led to the siege of the latter in 1649.

In the same year, shortly after the execution of Charles I, the presbytery of Belfast published what it called *A Necessary Representation*, condemning the King's murder and other actions of the English Parliament, and declaring its support for the Solemn League and Covenant. The political opinions of an obscure group of Presbyterian ministers, in a remote part of the British Isles, might swiftly have been forgotten had it not been for an unusual (and from their point of view very unfortunate) circumstance. Parliament decided to answer these accusations, and called upon the Latin Secretary to draft the reply. The Secretary was none other than John Milton, and for a brief moment his scorching invective lighted upon 'the blockish presbyters of Clandeboye'; their pamphlet and his reply to it are preserved in Milton's collected prose works, and are now part of the treasury of English letters.

For the historian, however, their chief interest lies in what they reveal about Presbyterian political attitudes and English reactions to them. In many ways, of course, *A Necessary Representation* was atypical. The very complicated circumstances of the Civil War had placed these Ulster Presbyterians in the unwonted situation (as a consequence of their support for their Scottish brethren) of taking the side of the monarchy against Parliament. But the whole of the *Representation* is instinct with the Presbyterian traits of independence, self-righteousness, criticism of civil government and even mistrust of religious toleration. Parliament was roundly condemned for endeavouring 'to establish by lawes an Universall Toleration of all religions, which is an Innovation overturning of Unity in Religion, and directly repugnant to the word of God', and for encouraging those who 'invent damnable errors, under the specious pretence of a Gospel-way, and New Light'. 'When we consider these things,' the presbytery asserted, 'we cannot but declare and manifest our utter dislike and detestation of such unwarrantable practices, directly subverting our Covenant, Religion, Lawes and Liberties. And as Watchmen in Sion warne all lovers of truth, and well-affected to the Covenant, carefully to avoid compliance with, or not bearing witness against horrid insolencies.'[9]

'What meane these men?' asked Milton in his reply. 'Is the Presbytery of Belfast, a small Town in Ulster, of so large extent that their voices cannot serve to teach duties in the Congregation which they oversee, without spreading and divulging to all parts farr beyond the Diocesse of Patrick or Columba, their written representation, under the suttle pretense of Feeding their own Flock.' For him Belfast was 'a barbarous nook in Ireland', a place 'whose obscurity till now never came to our hearing', and its Scottish ministers were 'unhallowed priestlings', 'a generation of High-land theevs and Red-shanks, who beeing neighbourly admitted, not as the Saxons by merit of thir warfare against our enemies, but by the courtesie of England to hold possessions in our Province, a Country better than thir own, have, with worse faith then those Heathen, prov'd ingratefull and treacherous guests to thir best friends and entertainers'.[10]

Milton's chief tactic was to implicate the Scottish ministers in the Irish rebellion. He seized upon this as the weakest point in their position, that they had now become accomplices and assistants to the Catholic Confederates of Kilkenny, their 'Copartning Rebels in the South, driving on the same Interest to loose us that Kingdome, that they may gaine it themselves, or at least share in the spoile: though the other be op'n enemies, these pretended Brethren'. There wanted but 'a few formall words, which may be easily dissembl'd, to make the perfetest conjunction; and betweene them to divide that Iland'.

To Milton there was little distinction between these presbyters and the Irish papists. He was indignant that they should brand Parliament with extirpation of laws and liberties, 'things which they seem as little to understand as ought that belongs to good letters or humanity'. Though they would be thought Protestants, they took sides with the Irish, and though they called themselves 'British', they criticized the actions of the English Parliament. Milton naturally makes a clear distinction between loyalty to the monarch and loyalty to England. (So do Ulster Protestants today, making the opposite choice from his.) Allowing for the special, and very different, circumstances in which these words were written, one cannot but be struck by their similarity to the kind of things Englishmen say about Ulster now. Why should they bother to distinguish between two different kinds of Irish? One lot is as bad as the other. Papist, Protestant or Presbyterian, they are all Irish, and everyone knows what that means. Milton relates their shortcomings with some relish. The Irish are a thoroughly inferior people, savage, inhumane, treacherous and ignorant. And even while he is writing, 'newes is brought, and too true, that the Scottish Inhabitants of that Province are actually revolted, and have not only besieged in London-Derry those Forces which were to have fought against the Irish Rebels; but have in a manner declar'd with them, and begun op'n war against the Parliament; and all this by the incitement and illusions of that unchristian Synagogue at *Belfast*.'[11]

The Presbyterian facility for getting on the wrong side of the establishment, even a revolutionary establishment which had itself just overthrown the monarchy and the institutions of state, is well illustrated by the episode. In this instance, the roles of authority and dissent were to some degree reversed, but the pattern remained the same; the Presbyterians were against the government. That tradition complicates the part which they have played in Irish history, and is the source of much confused thinking about the Northern Ireland problem.

The Presbyterians' relations with the new Commonwealth were at first no easier than those they had enjoyed with Parliament, for they continued to give qualified support to the cause of Charles II —a loyalty that was later to be ill rewarded. Cromwell was for a while well disposed to them, but inevitably he became more suspicious of their royalism. The Engagement Oath of 1650 required those who had taken the Covenant 'to renounce the pretended title of Charles Stewart, and the whole line of the late King James', and to be faithful to the Commonwealth. Once more the Presbyterians refused to take an oath against their consciences. Ministers were imprisoned or driven to Scotland, and in 1653 they were officially banished from Ireland. Cromwell even considered the wholesale transplantation of the Presbyterians to Tipperary, where they would not be able to communicate with their friends in Scotland. What the effect of that plantation might have been on Irish history can only be imagined, but it was a long way to Tipperary, and the scheme was never implemented. When Cromwell's son Henry became Lord Deputy, he intervened on their behalf in 1654; the persecution ended, and they received a very favourable and generous treatment until the Restoration.

That event brought a return of persecution, though the Ulster Presbyterians had played an important part in the political manœuvres which brought Charles II back to his throne. The King acknowledged their loyalty to him, but he was powerless to prevent the bishops taking their revenge. 'Thus there came a black cloud over this poor Church,' wrote Adair, 'for the old enemies became bitter and triumphed over the outed ministers that they might get some advantage over them.'[12] Even the Lord Lieutenant, the Duke of Ormond, spoke of the Presbyterians suffering for their loyalty to the King, and now suffering under him.

James II's Declaration of Indulgence of 1687, suspending penal laws against Catholics and dissenters, promised a greater freedom of worship to the Ulster Presbyterians. When James's true policy became clear, however, they began to fear another 1641, a fear rendered the more acute because the Anglicans had accepted so completely the royal authority. Thus, although the Presbyterians might well have taken the King's side in the struggle after 1688, in the event they made common cause with the Church of Ireland, and proved the alliance in the siege of Derry. The menace of 1641 closed the Protestant ranks, a pattern that was to repeat itself again and again down to the present day.

## 3. Regium Donum

The Ulster Presbyterians had hoped, at the beginning of the new century, that the strenuous part which they had played in support of William III, and in particular in the siege of Derry, where they claimed to have outnumbered the Anglican defenders by fifteen to one, might be rewarded by increased security and toleration of the sect by the government and by the established Church. It was not to be. Such benefits as they received, the renewal of the royal grant (the *regium donum*), and the abrogation of the oath of supremacy in Ireland, derived from the goodwill of the King and the English Parliament. The Irish government did nothing for them at all. Attempts to give them legal security by Toleration Bills introduced in Parliament in 1692 and 1695 were adroitly thwarted by the bishops, who feared the Presbyterians, not as scattered congregations of dissenters, but as a potential rival establishment, since they predominated in the north-east of Ireland, and one which might, as in Scotland, eventually succeed in overthrowing the episcopal church.

With the accession of Queen Anne the situation of the Presbyterians became even less secure. The Test Act, passed in 1704, made the taking of the sacrament of communion according to the rites of the Anglican Church a condition of holding any office, civil or military, under the Crown. The Protestant dissenters, like the Catholics, were thus excluded from all influence in the government of Ireland, which, for most of the eighteeenth century, was to be a monopoly of the Protestant Ascendancy. The term 'Protestant Ascendancy' has a precise historical meaning, and it is absurd to speak of the Presbyterians as being, either then or since, a part of it. Nevertheless the bishops who so warmly supported the denial of civil rights to Presbyterians knew perfectly well that if at any time the Ascendancy was threatened by the Catholic majority, the Presbyterians would unite with them in defence of the Protestant religion. The Sacramental Test was not repealed until 1780, at a time when the northern dissenters were becoming conscious of their political power, and proving more than usually difficult to a government hard pressed by the revolt of the American colonies.

At the beginning of the century, therefore, the Presbyterians were in a difficult and anomalous relationship with the civil government. Legally they had no right to exist at all; in practice they enjoyed a grudging toleration. Yet the validity of their marriages and the right to burial after the usage of the Presbyterian Church were denied. They could not teach in schools, and they were compelled to serve as churchwardens. Ministers were forbidden to meet in presbytery, or even to preach, and fined £100 if they celebrated the Lord's Supper.

Not the least of the anomalies of the Presbyterians' situation was that, though they were not recognized by the law, they had received since the reign of Charles II a regular government grant to their clergy, known as the *regium donum*. Charles was supposed to have said that no Presbyterian could be a gentleman, but in 1672 he replied favourably to an approach by Sir Arthur Forbes on behalf of the dissenting clergy, and authorized an annual grant to them of £600. This grant was doubled by William III in 1690 in recognition of the Presbyterians' loyalty. It was briefly withdrawn at the end of Anne's reign, when the high Tories were ascendant, but George I restored it, and in 1718 he increased it by £400 per annum to the Synod of Ulster and £400 to Protestant dissenters in the south. In 1784 the *regium donum* paid to the Synod was increased to £2,600 and £500 was given to the Seceders,* and finally in 1792 it was increased to £5,000.

The *regium donum* was granted by the sovereign; it did not derive from Parliament or from the Irish government. Nevertheless, the Presbyterians cherished it as some kind of official recognition at a time when they were denied legal status as a church, and from the government's point of view it provided a kind of guarantee of loyalty. Since the dissenters were so touchy on the subject of Church–State relations, it was also the cause of frequent, and often very heated, wrangling. Part of the motive for augmenting the grant in 1792 was to try to restrain the Presbyterian clergy from the disloyal courses on which so many of them were just then embarking.

That course will be examined in greater detail in the following chapter, but for the sake of continuity the story of the *regium donum* may be completed. After the 1798 rebellion and the Union, the British government applied the principle once more. In 1803, on a plan of Lord Castlereagh's, the *regium donum* was substantially augmented, but this time the congregations were classified in three categories with differential rates of payment. This classification caused much bitterness, and brought to the surface once again all the old arguments. Henceforward the agent for the distribution of the grant was appointed and paid by the government, and the first to hold the position was Dr. Black, the leader of the conservatives in the Synod and Castlereagh's protégé. The ministers of the poorer congregations, who formed a majority in the Synod, were understandably chagrined at the scheme of differentiation, and raised the cry that Black was introducing a disguised form of prelacy, and that the *regium donum* was simply a bribe to make the clergy more amenable to the dictates of government. The principle of classification had been strenuously opposed in the Synods which met between its first enunciation in 1800 and its implementation in 1803, but the government refused to budge, and in the long run the clergy dared not refuse the augmentation even on these terms.

* See page 97 below.

Castlereagh was undoubtedly actuated, in the historian's words, 'by those purely secular considerations which ordinarily have weight with prudent and calculating statesmen',[13] for the theory was that the grant would render the Presbyterian clergy independent of their flocks in the troubled years following 1798. Indeed the calamitous results of the Presbyterians' involvement in radical politics partly explains the ease with which the Synod finally submitted. The voice of criticism was not silenced, however, and the motives of the government remained suspect. In another form, government intervention in the Synod's affairs was some years later to provoke one of the most dramatic speeches ever delivered in a Presbyterian assembly.

The Ulster Presbyterians, like their brethren in Scotland, placed a very high value on education. Most of the ministers received their academic training at the Scottish universities, and they had long endeavoured to establish a college in Ulster for the education of their clergy. In the last two decades of the eighteenth century, attempts to found academies for this purpose at Strabane, Armagh, Killyleagh and elsewhere proved abortive, but in 1785 one Dr. Crombie opened an academy on the Scottish model in Belfast, and its second headmaster, the eloquent and influential Dr. William Bruce, established its reputation. Bruce had led the moderate party in Belfast politics of the 1790s, and in 1806 members of the radical group associated with the United Irishmen set up a rival establishment, the Belfast Academical Institution. Both academies still exist, as leading Belfast schools, but the original intention of their founders was that one or other should come to be accepted as a seminary for the Presbyterian clergy and ultimately become a Presbyterian university. In the end it was to the Academical Institution that the Synod gave its blessing, and in 1815 the government, as part of its policy towards the Synod, provided an annual grant of £1,500.

The radical associations of the new institution were, however, to continue to cause embarrassment. On St. Patrick's Day, 1816, several radical toasts were drunk at a dinner attended by some of the board of managers, and Castlereagh made it clear that the grant might be withdrawn, and that the government did not look favourably on the Synod's proposal to elect a professor in the institution for the education of students in theology. A deputation which waited upon Castlereagh to try to mollify him was coldly received. It presented its report to a crowded Synod in Belfast in 1817. W. D. Killen, who completed J. S. Reid's *History*, declares that there was a prevailing impression throughout the house that a blow was being aimed at the independence of the Church, and that the Synod had reached the most important crisis in its history. But, while 'the senior members paused and hesitated' the Rev. James Carlile, the young minister of Mary's Abbey, Dublin, advanced to the pulpit, and electrified his brethren with a speech of which this is the peroration:

'There are, moderator, some proposals which may be made to individuals, or to public bodies, on which it is infamous even to deliberate. Such seems to me to be the nature of the proposal made to us at our late meeting in Cookstown, when, by a verbal message from an individual styling himself Lord Castlereagh, we were informed that government may regard our electing a professor for educating our students in theology as an act of hostility, and we were required to desist from our purpose. Who or what is this Lord Castlereagh, that he should send such a message to the Synod of Ulster? Is he a minister of the body? Is he an elder? What right has he to obtrude himself on our deliberations? I revere the government of my country. I pay it a willing obedience in matters civil. I am no cavilling politician. But I protest against government dictating an opinion as to the measures we should adopt for the interests of religion. As long as I can raise my voice, I will raise it against the principle of admitting civil governors, as such, to be heard in our deliberations. Where now is the high spirit of independence, the stern integrity of our ancestors, which would have made them walk steadily to the stake or to the gibbet before they would have suffered any civil magistrate to dictate to them where their students should be educated? . . . This day's decision will tell whether we deserve to rank as an independent, upright, conscientious body, with no other end in view than the glory of God and the welfare of His Church, or whether we deserve that Lord Castlereagh should drive his chariot into the midst of us, and tread us down as the offal of the streets.'[14]

The young pastor's address, says Killen, 'thrilled through

Presbyterian hearts, awakening the martyr spirit of olden time'.[15] It has been argued that Carlile's speech was less dramatic for his hearers than Killen makes it appear, and that other speakers accused him of being unfair to the government, which had not attempted to encroach on the rights and privileges of Presbyterians,[16] but, even if that is allowed, the tone of the speech, and Killen's treatment of it, reflect the essential independence of the Presbyterian attitude to civil government. His sentence—'whilst the senior members paused and hesitated, one of the young ministers had the moral courage to come forward and take the lead in repelling the aggression'—is deeply significant. We are once again watching the apprentices shut the gates of Derry.

# 4. New Light

One characteristic which Irish Presbyterianism inherited from the parent church in Scotland was a strong tendency to schism, the inevitable consequence of attaching so much importance to the right of individual conscience. There were in the eighteenth century, and there still are, Presbyterian congregations scattered throughout the other three provinces,* but for the most part the Presbyterians were concentrated in the north. The divisions which from time to time occurred in the Kirk of Scotland tended, like fault lines in the geological structure, to reappear on the Ulster side of the North Channel.

Thus the Reformed Church, which broke away because many of the Scottish Covenanters could not accept the Revolution Settlement of 1689–90, established itself in Ulster from the middle of the eighteenth century. Its adherents virtually refused participa-

* Many of the southern congregations were in origin congregations of Independents, created during Cromwellian times. Their connection with the Synod of Ulster was complicated and not easy to define. In 1696 Presbyterians and Independents combined to form the Presbytery of Munster. This body, together with some Dublin congregations, was to become generally known as 'the Southern Association'. (See Reid, *History*, vol. iii, p. 85n.)

tion in all civil government because the Settlement had recognized neither of the Covenants; and they found the soil of Ulster congenial. There they remained a minority, but their attitude to government had an important bearing on Presbyterian politics at the end of the century, and is not without influence still.

Another breakaway communion, that of the Associate Presbytery or Secession Church, arose from the disputes of 1712 in Scotland, when patronage was re-imposed upon the Church by Act of Parliament. It also gained a following in Ulster, and in 1747 it was itself divided by the controversy over the Burgess Oath in Scotland into 'Burghers' and 'Anti-Burghers'. None of these disputes had any relevance in Ireland, and they demonstrated not only the proximity of Scotland, but the Presbyterians' marked taste for religious disputation. This kind of outlook is still very strong in Ulster today, and it helps to explain the strength of feeling about, for example, ecumenical movements.

The most important and far-reaching schism, however, was a doctrinal one of indigenous origin, concerned with subscription to the Westminster Confession of Faith, which had been drawn up by an assembly of divines in 1643. The ministers who met in the first Presbytery of 1642, though they had all signed the Scottish Confession of 1560, entered their new livings without any subsequent subscription, and this tradition was continued. The Synod of Ulster, when it came into existence in 1690, operated on the same basis as the parent church in Scotland and accepted the same system of discipline and government. This was made easier by the fact that most of the ministers had been educated at the Scottish universities and had been licentiates of the Scottish Church. Both ministers and people were, in the words of the historian Reid, 'warmly attached to all its principles and usages, and, for the most part thoroughly instructed in the controversies by which their Church had from time to time been tried'.[17]

The Presbyterian Church could not remain immune to those latitudinarian influences which in the eighteenth century began to affect all denominations. In 1705 the Rev. John Abernethy, a young minister of the presbytery of Antrim, formed with some of his clerical colleagues a society which met once a month in Belfast to listen to sermons, debate theological matters, review books and pursue the textual study of the Scriptures. The Belfast Society was to exercise considerable influence in the Synod of Ulster between 1709 and 1716, providing five of its moderators, but in some quarters it was suspected of propagating opinions which had been adopted by Swiss Calvinists and certain English dissenters, and which were held to undermine orthodox Presbyterian doctrine and discipline. Its members openly expressed their opposition to the use of 'man-made' confessions as a test of orthodoxy; on the other hand, the charge that some of them had embraced the Arian heresy, by denying the doctrine of the Trinity, was hotly rejected by them, and was almost certainly untrue. Nevertheless, the label of Arian was to be applied to them throughout the long history of this and later controversies.

The question did not agitate the Synod until 1719, when Abernethy preached a sermon on 'Religious obedience founded on personal persuasion'. With its publication in 1720, a seven-year war of words began, in which scores of pamphlet broadsides were fired. In one of the earliest, the Rev. John Malcolm of Dunmurry, near Belfast, a staunch champion of orthodoxy, dubbed Abernethy's opinion 'New Light'. The term was not new (see p. 88) but henceforth it was to be used to describe the less orthodox, and often the more urbane and erudite, body of Ulster Presbyterians.

Two courses were open to the Synod. It might have brought the suspected brethren to trial for heresy, and either expelled them or cleared them of the imputation; or it might have obliged all new entrants to the Synod to subscribe to the Westminster Confession, and thus ensured orthodoxy for the future. Neither course was followed, and instead all the nonsubscribers were placed in the presbytery of Antrim. The presbytery parted from the Synod in 1726, but on surprisingly amicable terms. It retained a form of association with the Synod for another eighty years, and neither body denied its pulpits or its fellowship to the other, despite their doctrinal differences. Strangely, the Synod permitted nonsubscription to continue as before, thus nourishing the seeds of a second, and much more damaging, nonsubscription dispute in the nineteenth century.

The significance of the nonsubscription controversies is that they illustrate, in dramatic form, the inherent tension of Presbyterianism, between traditional ecclesiastical orthodoxy and the right of private judgement. This tension is found, of course, in all churches, but the democratic nature of Presbyterian church government makes it more sharply apparent. In each generation Presbyterianism has shown an almost Manichean duality of outlook, Old Light and New Light, fundamentalist and intellectual, extremist and moderate. During the second half of the eighteenth century the balance seemed to be moving slowly in favour of New Light opinions, and to a large extent this was a reflection of general attitudes to religion in the age of the Enlightenment. In the early nineteenth century, however, the balance moved sharply in the other direction. Evangelical religion triumphed, and after an epic nine-year controversy over subscription, the New Light and Unitarian ministers withdrew from the Synod in 1830.

In this great battle the respective parties had been led by two ministers of outstanding ability and strong personality, giants of religious disputation. At the head of the New Lighters was the Rev. Henry Montgomery, while the orthodox and conservative Presbyterians were led by Dr. Henry Cooke. When Montgomery and the Remonstrants (as they were called) withdrew from the Synod, the way was open for a union between it and the Seceders. This occurred in 1840, since when the governing body has been known as the General Assembly of the Presbyterian Church in Ireland.

The Church is likely to produce Cookes and Montgomerys in every age. On the whole there are more Cookes, for evangelical Presbyterianism will always have a broad popular support, while New Light views must of necessity be confined to a minority. The alternation between Old Light and New Light theology readily coincided with an even older pulse in the Presbyterian mind, that of revival and religious torpor. And New Light principles have generally been correlated with liberal politics, Old Light with conservative. It was Cooke, indeed, who proclaimed the banns of marriage between the Presbyterians and the traditionally conservative Anglicans in 1834, a move of great significance for the future of Irish politics. [This correlation was not absolute since the orthodox were often critical of government—a few of the United Irishmen, for example, were Old Light ministers.] There

is thus also a duality of political outlook among the Presbyterians, with the tide tending to run in favour of the Old Light men, who may be, as in the recent Northern Ireland crisis, the breakaway Presbyterians.

This dual outlook is often unsuspected by the outside observer, who may even mistake one group for the other. Thus many people outside Ulster have since 1969 assumed that the Rev. Ian Paisley, and not the Moderator of the General Assembly, is the head of the Presbyterian Church. Dr. Paisley is, of course, the founder and leader of a rapidly growing schismatic body, the Free Presbyterian Church. By immutable laws, this Church was bound to increase its strength enormously as Ulster Protestants became more and more threatened, either by Catholic nationalism or by the British government. This is the factor which makes it difficult to force the Ulsterman to adopt certain desirable political attitudes, in particular to see the virtue of compromise. Reason and instinct may pull in opposite directions, and instinct, which he will call conscience, will generally win.

Reid's account of the subscription controversies is itself an example of the way in which the Ulster mind works. Though he gives an accurate summary of the views of both sides, he makes no effort to be impartial. He indicates that the nonsubscribers, though sincere, were misguided, and that their theological errors were to lead them into the politics of rebellion, and to involve both them and Ireland in great and needless suffering. To be objective on such a matter as this would not be, in Reid's view, a scholarly virtue, but a sin against conscience. In his treatment of the Synod's attitude in 1720, he displays that desire for moral certainty which is so characteristic of the Ulster outlook on both politics and religion. He says, in effect, that the fathers of the Synod should have adopted almost any course rather than temporize or try to comprehend the suspected brethren. 'Better far would it have been for the interests of truth, the peace of the Church, and her future prosperity had either of the other two expedients been preferred [i.e. exclusion or the enjoining of subscription on new entrants]. It ought to be remembered, however, that the brethren whose counsels were followed by the synod had not had the experience which we now have of the fruitless results of all such temporizing expedients for preserving peace and unity, where important doctrinal differences exist.'[18]

These words have a familiar ring today. The same criticism is levelled by Ulstermen, Protestant and Catholic, against the kind of temporizing policies pursued by British governments in dealing with Northern Ireland's problems. Whereas the English believe that compromise is the answer to all disputes, Ulstermen believe the opposite. The resulting *mésentente* leads Ulstermen and Englishmen to despair of one another.

# 5. The Harp New-Strung

During the last quarter of the eighteenth century, the northern Presbyterians played a leading role in the drama of Irish history. Yet it was an enigmatic role, and one which may have been profoundly misunderstood by later generations. At the zenith of the political achievement of the so-called 'Protestant nation', there was formed, among the middle-class Presbyterians of Belfast, the radical society of United Irishmen, whose threefold aim was Catholic emancipation, the reform of Parliament and the independence of Ireland. The United Irishmen held the view that no reform or political progress was possible in Ireland until dissenter and Catholic united to isolate the Irish executive and overthrow the power of the Anglican Protestant Ascendancy. The age of the Protestant nation ended with the United Irish insurrection of 1798 and the Act of Union which followed it in 1800. Many of those Protestants who had spoken up most vociferously for the rights of Ireland then became fervent supporters of the British connection and left the national cause to the Catholic majority.

There can be no doubt that the Presbyterians were deeply implicated in the United Irish movement. The idea of an inner circle of dedicated constitutional reformers, patriots who would from behind the scenes direct Protestant politics into a single national effort, was first suggested by William Drennan, a Belfast

Presbyterian doctor of radical views (and not, as is almost universally believed, by Wolfe Tone). Drennan, the son of a New Light minister who had been the friend of the philosopher Francis Hutcheson, first outlined his plan in 1784, when the popular liberal movement was losing political momentum. It thus owed more in origin to the radical ferment caused by the revolt of the American colonies than to the French Revolution.

Nevertheless it was the latter event which translated idea into action. In 1791 Drennan revived his scheme (other reformers were now thinking along the same lines), and his friends, inspired by the news from France and the publication of Paine's *The Rights of Man*, formed a secret committee in Belfast. In the autumn this committee invited Wolfe Tone, a young Dublin barrister who had published a pamphlet in support of Catholic emancipation, to visit Belfast and help them to form a political association with Protestant and Catholic radicals in Dublin and elsewhere. Tone changed the name of Drennan's society from the Irish Brotherhood to the United Irishmen and drew up some of its first resolutions, in rivalry with Drennan. When a second cell of United Irishmen was formed in Dublin, Drennan became its president, and Tone admits that he almost at once lost any influence over its proceedings. By his subsequent actions, however, Tone fully earned his place in the pantheon of Irish patriots, and eclipsed the more cautious Belfast men who had been the society's founders.

The United Irish movement was thus a Presbyterian initiative. The first members were sons of the manse, and elders of congregations. More than a score of Presbyterian clergy were directly implicated in the rising of 1798, and of these four were executed and the rest banished to France and America. In the north, the main rank and file of the organization were Presbyterian tenant farmers from Antrim, Down and part of Londonderry. By its very nature the united movement sought the support of Irishmen of all religious persuasions. The composition of the Dublin society was much more diverse than that of the Belfast society and consisted mainly of Anglican and Catholic middle-class radicals. Beyond the two urban centres Catholic support was much harder to win than Presbyterian, and Catholics came into the United Irish ranks in large numbers only after 1795, when the

movement went underground and joined forces with the secret
agrarian society of the Defenders. The Defenders became United
Irishmen largely in reaction to the nascent Orange movement
among Protestants.

The apparent departure of the Belfast Presbyterians after 1791
from the traditional attitudes towards Catholics, Anglicans and the
connection with Britain, which they held before and since, cannot
be understood outside the context of Irish politics in the last
quarter of the eighteenth century. For most of the century the
politics of Ireland had seemed to flow placidly in safe and predictable channels, though it is fair to say that the earlier period only
seems to be uncomplicated because so few historians have chosen
to study it. All historical interest tends to be compound interest.
Those periods which have produced most books will produce
even more. On the other hand it is true that in 1775 events of
enormous consequence in the outside world produced political
turmoil in Ireland and ushered in a period of rapid and exciting
change.

The period between 1704 and 1775 in Ireland was the era of the
Penal Laws, that haphazard but effective accumulation of statutes
which collectively excluded the entire Catholic population from the
political and public life of the country, and further, interfered
with their rights to worship, or educate their children, as they
pleased, or to bequeath their property in the normal way. Such
codes of law directed against a particular religion were not peculiar
to Ireland, but in other countries, including England and France,
they operated against minorities and not against majorities. In an
age when politics still coincided with religion, they were judged on
practical expediency, and not on principles of abstract justice as
they would be today, so that it is not very illuminating to try to
see them in a post–eighteenth-century light.

Paradoxically they have been more resented by Catholics since
their repeal than they seem to have been by Catholics who lived
under them. This was in part because they were much more
stringent in the letter than in enforcement. Those laws which
affected worship, or the freedom of the clergy, and imposed irk-
some petty restrictions, were soon allowed to fall into desuetude
and were often circumvented by collusion with Protestants. But

those which buttressed the political power of the Ascendancy, that is, those which related to property, the parliamentary franchise and the right of election to corporations of boroughs, were vigorously applied.

As the century progressed, the Protestants began to feel more secure, especially as Catholics had shown no inclination to challenge the Ascendancy, or to support the Jacobite cause during the rebellions of 1715 and 1745 in Scotland. In such circumstances it was inevitable that there should develop within the Ascendancy the assertion of a colonial nationalism. The Protestant case for greater independence for Ireland grew from the forceful arguments of Molyneux and Swift, and matured slowly, revealing its existence in moments of constitutional crisis such as the 'Wood's Halfpence' affair of 1722–5 and the Money Bill disputes of 1753–6. As the Earl of Charlemont declared later, such controversies showed that Ireland had, or ought to have, a constitution of her own, and from the middle of the century onward there was always a nucleus of 'independent' members in the Irish House of Commons, who were identified as 'the patriots'.

The revolt of the American colonies gave a completely new complexion to Irish politics. When Ireland was denuded of troops to provide reinforcements for America, the way was left open for the creation of the Volunteers, a citizen militia recruited mainly from the Protestant middle class and led by the aristocracy. The Volunteers, enrolled for the ostensible purpose of defending the coasts of Ireland from invasion or isolated raids by privateers, had the secondary function of preserving order and guarding life and property if the volatile elements in the Irish population should be tempted to seize the opportunity to make mischief. The Volunteers were drawn from those ranks of Protestant society that felt their political influence was not commensurate with their economic importance. Raised in the first place to defend Ireland from foreign intervention, they became a great popular political movement which was in fact a rival to the unrepresentative Irish Parliament.

The American war affected the Presbyterians in a peculiarly close way, for during the eighteenth century there had been a steady stream of emigration from Ulster to the colonies, and by 1775 a majority of Presbyterians had family connections on the other side of the Atlantic. The Scotch-Irish, as they are called in the United States, played a not inconsiderable part in the American Revolution, and were well regarded by Washington, who said that if he were defeated everywhere else he would make his last stand among the Scotch-Irish of his native Virginia. The Ulster Presbyterians were therefore very sympathetic to the ideals of the colonists, and this reinforced their criticism of British government in Ireland.

Again, in 1775 the dissenters were still smarting under legal disabilities. Although they did not suffer as severely as the Catholics, they felt a keen resentment at their continued treatment as less than full citizens. The merchants, lawyers and doctors of Belfast resented their total exclusion from the government not only of their country but of their own town, for Belfast had a closed corporation under the control of Chichester's descendants, the Earls of Donegall. The Presbyterian middle class was intensely political and public-spirited, and the Volunteer movement gave it an unprecedented opportunity to put its views to a national audience.

The patriots, men such as Flood and Grattan, rapidly allied their cause with the Volunteer movement, and within a few years achieved most of their long-standing aims. Commercial restrictions were swept away in 1779. In 1782 the Declaratory Act (the famous '6 George I' which stated that the English Parliament had the right to legislate for Ireland) was repealed, and Ireland seemed to have achieved legislative independence. These changes were as much, or more, a consequence of political changes in England, brought about by the strains and disasters of the American war, but in Ireland it was felt that the culminating act in the Volunteer campaign, the great convention of Volunteer delegates held in Dungannon in February 1782 to demand reform, had given Ireland her new 'constitution'. The Volunteers were always thereafter to consider Dungannon as the high-water mark of their political achievement, and for many years to come they were to strive vainly to recapture the influence which they had enjoyed at that time.

The popular victory was more apparent than real because the new relationship between Britain and Ireland was never satisfactorily defined, and the independence of the Irish Parliament lasted only eighteen years. The alliance of aristocracy and middle-class did not survive the success of 1782. When the Volunteers went on to press for the much more divisive objectives of parliamentary reform and Catholic emancipation, the unanimity of Protestant nationalism dissolved.

It was in these circumstances of political frustration that the United Irish movement was born among the Belfast Presbyterians. By this time Belfast had acquired a reputation for being in the vanguard of the radical reform movement, but other elements of the Volunteers, in Co. Armagh, for example, and in Co. Londonderry, were much more conservative and anti-Catholic. Thus the Volunteer movement was, by a strange sequence of events, to provide recruits for both the United Irishmen and the Orange lodges.

What happened in Belfast in 1791 has created a legend in Irish history, the legend that the Presbyterians and Catholics completely forgot their long history of sectarian hostility and joined in a national effort to free Ireland from English rule. At first constitutional, this activity became secret and revolutionary, and in 1798 dissenter and Catholic rose in rebellion and fought side by side against the British army for French democracy and Irish freedom. At Antrim, at Saintfield and at Ballynahinch the Presbyterians marched under the green flag with the Irish harp, and sang the 'Marseillaise' and the 'Shan Van Vocht' (the poor old woman who was Ireland):

> Oh the French are in the bay,
> They'll be here by break of day,
> Says the Shan Van Vocht,
> And Ireland shall be free,
> From the centre to the sea,
> Says the Shan Van Vocht.

This poses one of the most puzzling questions in Irish history. Why did the northern Presbyterians, who had been nationalists and radicals in 1798, so quickly become unionists and conservatives thereafter? The more closely we examine the whole pattern, however, the less sharp the antithesis appears.

In the first place it is simply not true that the Presbyterians as a body held radical opinions between 1790 and 1800. Throughout the whole period the majority of ministers in the General Synod of Ulster was conservative, suspicious of Catholic political designs and critical of those Presbyterians who became infected with French revolutionary ideals. The records of the Synod mention the insurrection only to deplore it, and to censure the levelling and republican principles which brought it about. It must be remembered, too, that the Presbyterians' republicanism—this strange legacy they were to leave to the Catholic Ireland of later times—long predated the establishment of the French Republic, which is often popularly supposed to have been its origin, and was compounded of many ingredients peculiar to the dissenters' history. In 1787, two years before the Revolution broke out, we find the Lord Lieutenant, the Duke of Rutland, observing that 'the Province of Ulster is filled with dissenters, who are in general very factious—great levellers and republicans'.[19] And, as he goes on to remark, there were many sects of them, Old Light, New Light, Seceders, and so on. We must not assume that they all shared exactly the same political views.

We can easily forget, in making generalizations, that the Presbyterians were not totally nationalist in 1798 and totally unionist in 1886. The Presbyterian body exhibited a stratification of political views, some of the complications and cross-faults of which have already been discussed. It so happened in 1798 (or more accurately some years earlier) that the radical stratum came to the surface and was very prominently in view. For the moment, in the heady excitement of the French Revolution, the conservatives attracted less attention. In later times the conservative stratum was so obvious that the radical traditions inherent in Ulster Presbyterianism were completely forgotten. Indeed this is true today.

Though it does not, in the summary view, *seem* that the United Irishmen and their sympathizers were in a minority, this becomes quite clear when one looks at the problem from another point of view, the territorial one. The United Irishmen were drawn from a relatively small and well-defined area. Throughout Ireland as a whole, the political movement was sharply confined to the east, and specifically to the urban centres, Belfast and Dublin, the bases of middle-class radicalism. In the north, only Belfast and its hinterland in Antrim and Down produced United Irishmen in large numbers. We do not find much United Irish activity among the Presbyterians of Co. Tyrone or the Laggan area of Donegal. Even more remarkably, we do not find it in Co. Armagh, which was in the very forefront of Volunteer liberalism in the 1780s. The nature of the Presbyterian reaction to the United Irish philosophy depended on the balance of population between Protestant and Catholic and on a variety of local factors. Significantly, United Irish societies did not flourish in areas where Protestants had been massacred in 1641, and one of the most extreme anti-United Irish and anti-Catholic songs of 1798, 'Croppies lie down', has the lines

> *Remember the steel of Sir Phelim O'Neill*
> *Who slaughtered our fathers in Catholic zeal.*

In 1798, it is true, the rebellion was more widespread, and this indicates another source of confusion about the United Irishmen. Although the insurrection has gone down in the history books as a planned United Irish attempt to overthrow British rule in Ireland, it was at the same time more, and less, than this. In its most horrific and dramatic aspects it was a kind of *jacquerie* in which powerful social and economic grievances mixed and interacted with well-recognized patterns of endemic guerrilla war, which are considered in the following chapters.

Secondly, because the very foundation of the United Irish political programme was that Catholic and Protestant should unite to reform or overthrow a corrupt government, it is natural to assume that Protestant United Irishmen had completely overcome their attitudes of distrust towards Catholics. This is far from being the case, and there was in fact some ambivalence in their political outlook. By the same token, the efforts made by Catholic radicals (who formed a smaller minority in the entire Catholic body than the radical dissenters did in the Presbyterian) to form a political alliance with Presbyterians and Anglicans do not mean that they had abandoned their traditional attitudes to Protestant planters.

The correspondence of Dr. Drennan is full of references to his distrust of Catholic political motives. In particular, he suspected that the Catholic radicals wished to achieve Catholic emancipation

by having 'two strings to their bow', on the one hand by giving
loyalty to the British government in order to obtain redress from
that source, thus short-circuiting the Protestant Ascendancy, and
on the other, by joining hands with the Protestant radicals to overthrow the Irish government and frighten London with the spectre
of Protestant and Catholic united in an Irish revolution. This was,
of course, the strategy of the Catholic Committee, and some of its
members deliberately joined the United Irish society to increase
the committee's leverage in negotiating directly with Pitt. Drennan
admits that this is 'good, and perhaps fair, archery'[20] but he fears
too that it might mean the ultimate isolation of the New Light
dissenters.

Thirdly, almost everyone has tended to assume, like the United
Irishmen themselves, that because unity was proclaimed, it was
also in some way achieved. But a closer look at the texture of
northern society at this time shows unmistakably that this was not
true. No hiatus in fact occurred in the centuries-old strife between
the religious sects; if anything, sectarian tension increased at this
time. The entire United Irish movement, and the rebellion of
1798, have to be seen against a background of violence which
shows all too clearly the vitality of these religious animosities
which the United Irishmen so much deplored. The orange did
not decay, as the *Shan Van Vocht* had hoped, but grew riper every
day, and the Defenders had more Catholic recruits than the
radical societies.

In their hearts, the United Irish leaders knew this well enough.
One does not have to look beyond the *Autobiography* of Wolfe
Tone to find accounts of the powerlessness of the United Irish to
stop clashes between dissenter and Catholic in Rathfriland in
Co. Down.[21] One very good reason for this was, of course, that
the United Irish leaders were urban middle class, and the disturbers of the peace were agrarian workers. Historians enthusiastic
for the United Irishmen, and the republican nationalism which
they represented, have often ignored this obvious evidence of
failure, but in any event a great deal of evidence on patterns of
conflict is only now being evaluated.

The basic dilemma which confronted the United Irishmen was
this: they believed that Protestant and Catholic should unite to

achieve their political aims, but many of them became convinced (especially after the frustrating Fitzwilliam episode of 1795, when a liberal-minded lord lieutenant was abruptly recalled for showing too much sympathy to the emancipation cause) that only by insurrection could reform be secured. The repression of the movement by the government, forcing it underground, reinforced this tendency. But, since the failure of their basic strategy soon became apparent, they had to recruit potential insurgents from the ranks of the secret agrarian societies, whose very existence proved that sectarian strife was a much stronger tradition than unity.

Thus large numbers of Catholic Defenders were brought into the movement after 1796, and many of these took the field in 1798. It was hardly surprising, therefore, that 1798 witnessed scenes of sectarian massacre, notably in Wexford, and that the United Irish rebellion, as it is called, was in so many respects the antithesis of everything that the United Irishmen had stood for in 1791. The killing of Protestants on Wexford Bridge and at Scullabogue had an immediate effect on northern Presbyterian opinion, reviving all the fears of 1641. These fears had indeed intensified before 1798. To understand why, we must now turn to the strange laws which govern and direct Irish violence.

# PART FOUR

# Patterns of Conflict

# 1. Landscape with Bandits

The problem of violence in Irish history has not yet received the study it deserves. Most historians have been content to assume that it is generated by the deplorable circumstances of Irish history, and in particular by 'bad colonial government', the oppression of the Irish people by England. Yet this is a very sweeping assumption, and the evidence to support it is a good deal thinner than is generally imagined. One might just as easily assume that the Irish have been made violent by some noxious element in the potato, but of course no one would believe it, even if it were true. And it could just as well be argued that Irish history and Anglo-Irish relations have been tragic because the Irish are a violent and intemperate people.

Violence would appear to be endemic in Irish society, and this has been so as far back as history is recorded. Contrary to common belief, this violence is present during those periods of Irish history which stretch between the more dramatic outbreaks recorded in the history books. Even for the last two hundred years, it is only when one turns to the newspapers that the sheer intensity and continuity of disturbance becomes apparent. There can hardly be a square inch of earth anywhere in Ireland that has not been at some time stained with blood.

What has always been noted about the Irish is their capacity for very reckless violence, allied to a distorted moral sense which magnifies small sins and yet regards murder as trivial. Their kindness and hospitality are legendary, but so too is their reputation for hypocrisy and cruelty. It is sometimes argued that the moral distortion is the consequence of the troubles in the earlier part of the twentieth century, when terrible atrocities were committed during the Anglo-Irish war and the civil war. This cannot be true, because these same qualities are explicitly described in some of the earliest accounts of the Irish; it would seem far more likely that the frightfulness of the crimes committed in modern Ireland is to be explained by patterns of behaviour which are of great antiquity.

There is no lack of testimony on the peculiarities of the Irish attitude to violence. One clerical observer, as far back as 1566, recorded, with dubious syntax, that the Irish 'are of the opinion that neither violence, robbery nor murder is displeasing to God. If it were, they say, God would not tempt them with an opportunity.'[1] Over a century later, Eachard's *Exact Description of Ireland* describes the same trait in almost the same words: 'They also suppose that Violence and Murder are no ways of displeasing to God, for if it were a sin, he would not present them with that opportunity: further they say that this sort of life was left to them, and that they only walk in their Fathers' steps, that it would be a disgrace to their Nobility to forbear such Facts and get their living by Labour.'

Eachard noted that they were 'prodigal and careless of their lives', kind and courteous to strangers but 'impatient of abuse and injury, in enmity implacable, and in all affections most vehement and passionate'. Like most other observers he found that they were 'much delighted with Musick, but especially with the harp and Bagpipe', and that their funeral customs were unusual. When someone died, the women kept 'a Mourning with lowd Howlings and clapping of Hands together. When the Corps go forth they follow it with such a Peal of Out-Crys that a Man would think the quick as well as the Dead, were past all Recovery.' This practice of keening is accurately described by the English from the sixteenth century onward. Eachard adds that they mourned just as much for those slain in battle or by robbing, yet 'they will rail on their Enemies with Spiteful Words, and continue for a long time a deadly Hatred against all that Kindred'.[2]

Writing to a friend in 1750 John Wesley remarked that 'murder is a venial sin in Ireland'.[3] In 1825 Sir Walter Scott declared that the Irish 'will murther you on slight suspicion and find out the next day that it was all a mistake and that it was not yourself they meant to kill at all'.[4] Ten years later the German traveller J. G. Kohl noted the difficulty of carrying the law into force in Ireland, 'where so large a proportion of the population, even where they do not lend a hand to the murder, at all events sympathise with the murderer'.[5] These examples might be multiplied, but they are sufficient to illustrate the observation of traits which are clearly recognizable in modern Ireland.

Much less attention has been paid to the regularity of the forms in which Irish violence is expressed. Irish newspapers, the most useful source of information on this subject since the eighteenth century, carry column after column of detailed description of outrage and disturbance, even in years usually considered to be peaceful. A careful examination of such accounts soon reveals that the majority of these incidents have common characteristics, features which may not always be explicable in terms of the actual episode itself, but are part of larger patterns of behaviour. Each incident is like a piece of jigsaw, and the whole picture is revealed only when all the pieces are joined together.

Social historians have been vaguely aware of these patterns for a long time; political historians virtually ignore them. Much interesting information is still to be found in the accounts of those late eighteenth- and early nineteenth-century travellers with a sharp eye for Irish social customs. The formal patterns of agrarian outrage become clearly visible in the eighteenth century, but they were not new then; they can be traced back to the disturbed state of Ireland at the end of the seventeenth century, and beyond that to the rebellion and civil war of the 1640s. Their essential elements are already found in the sixteenth century, and even earlier.

The primary pattern which emerges from the background of Irish violence is that of the secret army, the shadowy banditti 'on their keeping' in the mountains and bogs, whose lineage is traceable from the woodkerne of the sixteenth century to the Provisional I.R.A. The text and woodcuts in John Derricke's *Image of Ireland*, published in 1581, depict activities startlingly similar to those which are still occurring in the twentieth century. Under a picture of the kerne setting fire to a farmhouse, Derricke's verses tell us that these are 'a packe of prowling mates' who 'spare no more their country byrth, than those of th' English race'.

*They spoile, and burne, and beare away, as fitte occasion serue,*
*And thinke the greater ill they doe, the greater prayse deserue;*
*They pass not for the poore mans cry, nor yet respect his teares*

*But rather joy to see the fire, to flash about his eares.*
*To see both flame, and smouldering smoke, to duske the christall*
*    skyes.*
*Next to their pray, therein I say, their second glory lyes.*[6]

Time and again, in describing the woodkerne, English observers remarked on the difficulty of coming to grips with them. After a raid on the planters' dwellings they simply melted away into the woods, or were metamorphosed into contented peasantry tilling the land or herding cattle. Long before Mao Tse-tung expressed his thoughts on fish swimming in water, they understood the principle well enough. We can trace their clandestine existence through the years of the plantations, the rebellion of 1641 and the war which followed. They were active in the disturbed period just before the Williamite war at the end of the seventeenth century, though their exploits have been overshadowed by more momentous events.

It was not until the eighteenth century, however, that they really got into the history books. They were those whom the local populace always referred to, cautiously but sympathetically, as 'the boys'—Whiteboys, Oakboys, Steelboys, Rightboys, the Boys of Wexford (1798 rebels), Peep o'Day Boys, Orange Boys. To this day in Ireland a local reference to 'the boys' will generally be taken to mean the I.R.A. (or whatever terrorist group is supported in the area). The Irish meaning of 'boy' thus retained something of its Elizabethan connotation as a swaggerer, a warrior, an armed man.

The secret armies were commanded by self-styled 'captains', a fashion which may have derived from the age-old customs of rustic festivities, for the Mayboys, Wrenboys and Strawboys also elected 'captains'. One Whiteboy declared before his execution: 'I acted one night among them as Captain, such as the Mayboys have.'[7] The captains chose graphic names, such as Lightfoot, Slasher, Cropper, Echo, Fearnot, Burnstack, Starlight, Dreadnought, Rock, Right, and so on. This custom was still followed at the period of the land war in the late nineteenth century. In 1881 Parnell warned the British government that if he were imprisoned, Captain Moonlight would take his place. The use of these pseudonyms, to preserve anonymity and to frighten potential victims, is a marked feature of more recent troubles. Statements issued to the press by clandestine terrorist groups are nearly always signed by a fictitious 'Captain'.

Sometimes the Whiteboys and their imitators issued threatening notices in the names of strange mythical female personages—Sieve Oultagh, Joanna or Shevane Meskill. They called themselves Sieve's children or 'sons to that poor old woman called Terry's Mother'.[8] This practice of issuing the threatening notice is itself very characteristic. The house of a potential victim was 'papered', by fixing on it a notice giving him what was considered fair warning to desist from the action which aroused their ire. To a remarkable degree, the I.R.A. and other terrorist groups still follow this practice, and indeed the whole barbarous process of intimidation in Belfast and elsewhere since 1969 can only be understood in relation to long folk-memories of how such things are done.

The Whiteboys (in Irish *Buachaillí Bána*) first appeared in 1761 in Co. Tipperary. They took their name from the white shirts which they wore over their clothes on their nocturnal expeditions, and they were also called Levellers because they pulled down the fences round enclosures. 'The disturbances of the Whiteboys,' wrote Arthur Young, 'which lasted ten years, in spite of every exertion of legal power, were in many circumstances very remarkable; and in none more so than the surprising intelligence among the insurgents wherever found . . . the numbers of bodies of them, at whatever distance from each other, seemed animated with one soul; and not an instance was known in that long course of time of a single individual betraying the cause; the severest threats, and the most splendid promises of reward, had no other effect but to draw closer the bands which connected a multitude, to all appearance so desultory.'[9]

Two similar agrarian armies appeared in Ulster at the same time. The Oakboys, also known as the Greenboys and the Hearts of Oak, became active in 1763 in Co. Tyrone, protesting against tithes and the county cess (or rates). They were provoked by the increased burden imposed by the building of new roads and by the attempts of Church of Ireland rectors to get full value in the tithes, and it is interesting that the immediate causes of these combinations were greater prosperity and a change in traditional dues (see p. 121 below). The Steelboys, or Hearts of Steel, came into existence after 1767 among tenants who suffered from the re-leasing of large parts of the estate of Lord Donegall in Co. Antrim, but they appeared in Co. Armagh and elsewhere as well. Both the Oakboys and the Steelboys were Protestant, and the latter were for the most part Presbyterian. The Whiteboys, though originally mixed in religion, soon became entirely Catholic. The Oakboy and Steelboy disturbances were of relatively short duration, but sporadic outbreaks of Whiteboy activity continued until the late 1780s.

Such organizations were able to mount a formidable threat to established order. A typical activity was the nocturnal attack on 'the big house' or the isolated substantial farm, so much a part of the Irish tradition from the sixteenth century onwards that most houses were perpetually in a state of readiness for siege. This helps to explain why the burning down of the Ascendancy big houses was a favourite recreation of the I.R.A. between 1920 and 1923. The purpose of such raids was usually to search for arms. Robbery was rarely the motive, and the occupants were not often murdered or in any way harmed, unless they fell into one of the dehumanized categories such as land agents or magistrates, who could expect no mercy. The latter were sometimes victims because they had taken strenuous action against members of the secret army. In 1775, for example, Ambrose Power, a Co. Tipperary magistrate and landlord, was murdered in his house at Barretstown, ostensibly for his part in arresting a local Whiteboy who called himself Captain Slasher. The real reason for his murder was probably that he had been active in the prosecution, ten years earlier, of Father Sheehy, a Catholic priest who was executed on trumped-up charges connecting him with Whiteboy outrages.

Dr. William Hamilton, a Church of Ireland rector and the author of *Letters concerning the Northern Coast of the County of Antrim*, was murdered in 1798 because, as a magistrate, he had been active in rounding up insurgents in Co. Donegal. Lecky describes his death thus: 'Dr. Hamilton had been from home for some days on business, and on his return he stopped at the house of a clergyman named Waller, who, like himself, had been a fellow of Trinity College, and who was now the rector of a parish halfway between Derry and Letterkenny, and six miles from Raphoe. In the evening he was sitting playing cards with the family of his host, when the house was attacked. Mrs. Waller was shot dead. Hamilton fled to the cellar, but the marauding party declared that they would burn the house, and kill everyone in it, unless he was given up. A man and two women servants dragged him from his place of concealment. He clung desperately to the staple of the hall-door lock, but the application of fire compelled him to loose his hold. He was thrust out, and in a moment murdered, and his body hideously mangled.'[10]

Like every other form of Irish disorder, such raids had strict conventions. A servant in the house who was sympathetic to the 'boys', and who might actually join them in attacking another property, would often stoutly defend his own house, even in his master's absence. A striking example of this in the mid-nineteenth century is given by A. M. Sullivan in his book *New Ireland*; and it is one worth quoting because it exhibits many other characteristics of the secret army tradition.

'The house of a Protestant gentleman farmer near Cashel was attacked, of all days in the year, on a Christmas-day. The gentleman himself was away in Dublin; and the place was in the charge of his son, aged twenty, and a servant-boy named Gorman. A servant-girl saw a party of men coming up the lawn, and, guessing their errand, she rushed in and gave the alarm. Gorman recognised them well enough. He had been "out" with them many a night on similar work; but now he was in charge of "the master's property", and he would defend it. He and young Fawcett barricaded the hall door and windows. Some of the assailants got in through the rear of the house, but a cross-door in the hall barred their way to where the guns which they wanted were kept. This they sought to force; Gorman expostulating and threatening to fire. They seem not to have credited this, and persisted, when, finding the door likely to yield, he aimed through a small fan-light at the top and mortally wounded the chief assailant, a young man named Buckley. The party fled, carrying their disabled leader; but eventually they found that escape was impossible with a wounded man, streaming with blood, in their arms. What were they to do? They hid him in some brushwood near a running stream, telling him on no account to make a noise, and promising that they would return for him at night. He endured great agony from thirst, and his resolution giving way, he cried aloud for water. Some women coming from Mass heard the moans, and discovering where he lay, brought him some water in his hat. This done, he implored them to "pass on", and say nothing. They knew what was meant, and silently went their way.'[11]

That night his companions returned with a door on which to bring him home, but he died on the way. They then concealed the body in a brake, setting watches to guard it day and night until it could be secretly buried. By now a strong force of police had arrived and begun to make a house to house search for the wounded man. Gorman, who had shot Buckley and knew him well, declared that the assailants were utter strangers. The gang raised fifty pounds for Buckley's mother, and broke to her the news of her son's death; she told the police that he had gone to seek work near Cahir. Buckley had a grand midnight funeral, but the local magistrate got to hear of it and with the police set out to disinter the body and examine it. An hour before they reached the grave-yard, the coffin was dug up and taken to the mountains. The chase after the corpse lasted two months; it was said to have been exhumed and reburied four or five times in all, before the search was called off and Buckley was brought back to rest in his father's grave at Ballyshehan. Some months later the magistrate was shot dead in his own house. Macabre incidents not unlike this have occurred more than once during the most recent I.R.A. campaigns in the north.

These highly formalized modes of agrarian violence persisted throughout the nineteenth century. The unwritten code was sometimes enforced by individuals or groups of peasants, but more often by the sworn members of one or other of the secret agrarian societies. Although they were known by many names—Blackfeet, Black Hens, Caravats, Carders, Lady Clares, Molly Maguires, Righters, Riskavallas, Rockites, Shanavats, Terry Alts, Thrashers and Whitefeet—they were generally called Ribbonmen, a slightly misleading designation since the Ribbon movement proper was largely confined to the north of Ireland, where it emerged as a Catholic answer to the Orange societies.

In 1836, in *On Local Disturbances in Ireland*, the first thorough
contemporary study of agrarian crime, George Cornewall Lewis
drew attention to some of the curious aspects of this secret war.
In particular, he observed that the worst violence occurred not, as
one might expect, in the poorest parts of Ireland, where economic
conditions were harsh, but in the fertile and more affluent regions.
'The disturbances in question', he wrote, 'appear to prevail most
where the peasantry are bold and robust, and one degree removed
above the lowest poverty; and where the land is productive. . . .
Thus one of the most disturbed districts in Ireland is that singu-
larly fertile plain which extends from Cashel into the county of
Limerick; indeed the southern part of the county of Tipperary
appears, from the very beginning, to have been remarkable for its
disturbances.'

Lewis's observations did not bear out the traditional view of
Irish peasants as a feckless and volatile race, degraded by poverty
and turning to violence through sheer desperation. On the contrary, they were a class 'remarkable for their patient endurance';
they were not temperamentally disposed to rebel but desired
rather that the status quo should be preserved. Under poverty,
failure of crops and scarcity of food they remained passive. What
drove them to outrage was invariably 'some active interference,
either actual or apprehended . . . some positive ill usage or
infliction of evil, such as ejectment from land, driving for rent,
etc. . . .'[12] The motives and tactics of outrage were then, and still
are today, often far removed from the idealistic conceptions of
nationality associated with them in the popular mind. The
Ribbonmen, as Professor Lee writes, 'had as little in common with
antiquarian dreamers wishing to restore a putative medieval
Gaelic commonwealth as they had with continental banditti. . . .
They pursued a limited, concrete, pragmatic programme. Indeed
the relentless realism of the Ribbon mind contrasts starkly with
the traditional picture of an impulsive, feckless peasantry living
in a mythical world of ancestral glories.'[13]

It is worthwhile to reflect on the extent of the injury which
these pragmatic terrorists could inflict on the authorities. In the
twenty years *before* the Famine nearly one hundred policemen
were killed and five hundred wounded in suppressing secret

societies. Although the agrarian societies challenged law and order in the state, their actions often reflected an excessive respect for lawful forms. They demanded absolute obedience to 'the law', but by this they meant their own unwritten law, which demanded among other things that you did not take land from which a tenant had been evicted, or buy confiscated cattle, or assist legal actions against tenants—as a process server, for example—or betray a member of the societies to the authorities. The legal form of threatening notices, which is so marked a feature of this clandestine activity, shows that they believed justice to be on their side, 'though they knew that the law was against them'.[14]

## 2. The Mills of Louth

Many of these characteristics are vividly illustrated in W. Steuart Trench's book *Realities of Irish Life*, which was published in 1868. Trench, who appears as an intelligent and humane land agent, relates that shortly after he took up his duties on the Marquess of Bath's estates in Co. Monaghan in 1851 he was warned by the tenants that the Ribbon conspiracy had determined to put him 'out of the way'. A magistrate and land agent named Mauleverer had been barbarously murdered a short time before at Crossmaglen in Co. Armagh, and Trench took the warning very seriously. At length he was informed that he had been formally tried by 'a judge and jury' in a large barn belonging to one of the tenants, and found guilty of being 'an exterminator'. Trench protected himself with great courage and ingenuity. Observing that the assassins of land agents generally escaped from the scene because those present invariably rushed to the aid of the victim, he never ventured forth without two armed men in attendance, with fixed orders that they were to pursue and apprehend his attackers without regard to him. He took care that these instructions reached the ears of the Ribbonmen, and he was never once attacked, although he subsequently learned that the conspirators had often been concealed in the hedges as he rode by.

Months later, when the ringleaders were arrested and tried for the murder of another agent, one of the accused, named Thornton, gave Trench a graphic and detailed account of the conspiracy. According to Thornton, Trench's trial *in absentia* had begun, after some serious drinking, with a curious ritual defence in which each tenant said something in his favour, in this way. The first one said:

'He gave me an iron gate.'

'May your cattle break their necks in it!' replied the president.

'He gave me slates and timber to roof my house,' said another.

'May the roof soon rot and fall!' replied the president. When this charade had continued for some time, the president pronounced him guilty. 'Boys, he *must die;* and now let us draw lots for the one that will do it.' The two assassins had already been elected, however, and they were now introduced. Neither of them lived on the estate, and neither knew Trench or had been injured by him. More liquor was brought in to celebrate the election. 'Many wild and exciting stories were told of landlords and agents who had been murdered, of the plots and contrivances by which they had been successfully waylaid, of the hairbreadth escapes of the "boys who had done it" and many jokes were passed at the victims being so suddenly "sent to hell"!'

The discussion then took a significantly historical turn. 'They say', observed one of the leaders, 'that if the boys had held out well when they rose in 1641 they could have had the country to themselves, and driven every Saxon out of it.' When someone remarked that the land laws were the real source of grievance, the president cried: 'A curse upon the land laws. . . . It's the *land itself* we want, and not all this bother about the laws. The laws is not so bad in the main, barrin' they make us pay rent at all. What good would altering the laws do us? sure we have tenant-right, and fair play enough, for that matter, for Trench never puts any one off the land that's able to pay his rent, and stand his ground on it. *But why should we pay rent at all?* That's the question, say I. Isn't the land our own, and wasn't it our ancestors' before us, until these bloody English came and took it all away from us? My curse upon them for it—but we will tear it back out of their heart's blood yet.'

After much more in this vein the president reached his peroration. 'Down with the Church [i.e., the Protestant Church of

Ireland], down with the landlords, down with the agents, down with everything, say I, that stands in the way of our own green land coming back to us again.'

'What wonderful grand fun we'll have fightin' among ourselves when it does come!' said a thick-set Herculean fellow at the lower end of the table.

'Well, now, I often thought of that!' replied his neighbour in a whisper. 'It'll be bloody work then in airnest, as sure as you and I live to see it. Anything that has happened up to this will be only a joke to what will happen then.'

'And what matter?' cried the advocate for fighting. 'Sure wouldn't it be far better any day to be fightin' among friends, than have no fightin' at all, and be slaves to our enemies?' The resident minstrel was then prevailed upon to sing the 'Shan Van Vocht', but before he did so he added some sombre thoughts of his own. 'They say the mills of Louth will turn round three times with blood before the land becomes our own again, but faix I often do be thinking it's our own blood will turn the wheel! and troth if that be the case I would sooner it stood still for many a twelve-month longer. . . . Man alive, you'll hear the people say that if Ireland would only rise against England in airnest, she'd soon show them she'd be free. But I tell ye they know nothing about it that says so. Ireland will never rise against England. *It's one half of Ireland must rise against the other half*—the Catholics who haven't the land against the Protestants who have. It would be hard to say which would win if they were left alone to fight it out between themselves, for the Protestants are terrible chaps for fightin' when they're put to it, and moreover some of the Catholics would join them. And then down comes England with her army of soldiers and all her cannon at her back to help the bloody Protestants, and what chance would the people have then?'

'It's too true,' replied the president. 'It's all too true entirely, but howld your tongue about that, and don't be putting it that way before the people. Wait till the big war comes anyway, and then we'll see what will turn up.'

'All right,' replied the minstrel. 'Leave it so; but mind I tell ye it's a worse look-out than many of ye think.'

The trial concluded with the president asking the elected assassins not to shoot Trench before the following Thursday, as the agent had promised to give him two iron gates for his farm that day. The party was about to break up, when someone asked if Trench ought not to be given fair notice. The president heatedly opposed such a suggestion, but it was eventually adopted, since it was 'the rule and the law', and on the next Sunday a general notice was posted at every Roman Catholic chapel in the area, warning all 'landlords, agents, bailiffs, grippers, process servers, and usurpers or underminers'.[15]

There are many curious aspects of this episode which cannot be connected directly with the actual circumstances of Trench's tenure of the agency. The attempt on his life was, he asserts, against the wishes of many of the tenants, who liked him and knew him to be a fair and liberal agent. He had not ejected a single tenant from the estate, and had accepted the agency only on condition that he should never have to turn anyone off the land, even for nonpayment of rent, without offering him a free passage to America and allowing him stock, crop and possessions, and the cancelling of all arrears. The 'president' of the secret court had admitted as much; in other words there was 'nothing personal' about his projected execution. But a considerable number of the tenants 'partly through terror established by the Ribbon conspiracy, and partly from a general feeling which then prevailed in the country, that all landlords and agents ought to be "put down" ', tacitly approved the action.[16]

The principle that 'all landlords and agents' ought to be murdered was thus well established long before the land war of 1879-80, and in the twentieth century it was applied to other groups—policemen, soldiers and government officials. Trench's would-be assailants were not so much reacting to his management of the estate as bringing certain patterns of violent behaviour to bear on an atmosphere of land agitation. Trench observed that particularly brutal murders had the opposite effect on the ill-disposed peasantry to that which might be expected. 'Having once, as it were, tasted blood, there was no crime that *some* of them were not ready to commit, to put down a landlord or an agent.'

Trench also noted that the ugly word 'murdered' was seldom used in Ireland when alluding to the killing of a landlord or agent.

Instead, the victim was 'put down', 'put out of the way' or 'put off the walk'. This persists to the present day: informers and enemies are 'executed', as if they had received a fair trial by judge and jury, and been found guilty of a capital offence. No doubt those who were involved in agrarian conspiracies often received scant sympathy from real judges and juries, but they seemed uncommonly anxious to imitate them; hence the charade of the secret trial, the ritual defence, announcing of the verdict and appointment of the executioners. The warning of the chosen victim was an essential feature of such activity, and the same sense of due process lies behind the disciplinary 'tarring', placarding and 'knee-capping' carried out by the Provisional I.R.A. and imitated by secret Protestant organizations today.

Equally significant was the fact that Trench's intended assassins were technically 'strangers' to the locality and did not know him personally. They had in fact to attend the petty sessions court in Carrickmacross, where he was sitting as a magistrate, in order to find out what he looked like. Money was raised to pay them for doing 'the job'. Trench was later able to study one of the men, Thornton, at close quarters while he was in prison and found him 'a weak small man, but clever and cunning to a degree'. He did not seem to be 'of a cruel or bloody disposition' but took a delight in waylaying and plotting. He told Trench, 'I never had any ill will in life to you at all,' and this was probably true.[17]

Another marked feature of this Ribbon trial was the frequent allusion to history and especially to land confiscation. The conspirators spoke of 1641 as though it had been a recent event. If only the 'boys' had held out well then, the land would have been in the right hands once more. 'I hear there was great sport up at the Castle at Carickmacross that time and that they put a rope round the agent's neck and were going to hang him at his own hall door.'[18] The vividness of Irish memory where confiscation was concerned has often been remarked. In his study of the 1870 Land Act, Dr. E. D. Steele remarks that the nineteenth-century antagonism between landlord and tenant 'was only partly—perhaps it was not even primarily—economic. It was rooted in the memory of the dispossession of the sixteenth and seventeenth centuries.' And he cites the example of John Blake Dillon, who in 1865 told a committee of the House of Commons that landlord-tenant relations were affected by 'very recent ... and very extensive confiscations'. Asked when these had taken place, he replied: 'In the time of Cromwell.'[19]

Trench remarks on the strong feeling among the Irish peasantry that the ancient families would yet recover the forfeited estates. The subject 'cropped up in many ways and on repeated occasions' in his dealings with the tenants. Maps were published and circulated showing the names of the original owners. This desire to recover the lost land is an important element in Protestant fears, and is a motif that appears frequently from the seventeenth century to the most recent Ulster crises.

Now it might reasonably be argued that Trench's account is not historical 'evidence' in the ordinary sense. We have only Trench's word for it that the episode was as Thornton told it to him, and Trench after all had also written a novel. The story doubtless received some literary embellishment, and the author intended the reader to be aware of the curious characteristics it illustrated, but two aspects of it point to its essential truth. The first is that even if Trench was inventing or elaborating the original, what he writes derived from his first-hand knowledge of his own tenants. Secondly, he could not have foreseen in 1868 the events of the twentieth century which so markedly fulfil the predictions of the man who said 'wait till the big war comes' or that once independence from England was achieved the Irish would fight one another. The 1916 Easter Rising occurred in the middle of the worst war the world had yet seen, and the Anglo-Irish war of 1919–21 was immediately followed by a civil war which was infinitely more cruel, though it occupies much less space, and often no space at all, in Irish history books. The mills of Louth were indeed to turn round three times with blood, and the blood of Irishmen, before the land became their own again.

# 3. Party Tunes

The emergence of the Ribbonmen in nineteenth-century Ireland was part of a complicated process which in the northern areas of the country had produced patterns of rural sectarian confrontation. The genesis of these encounters can best be seen in the events which led to the formation of the Orange Society and the growth of Defenderism in the last quarter of the preceding century.

Because the Orange institution has so often been held to be the cause of fomenting sectarian strife, it has long ago been forgotten that its birth was not the cause but the consequence of prolonged and severe sectarian conflict lasting for twenty years in a part of Co. Armagh. It used to be argued that Orangeism was born in Armagh because that was the county where Catholics and Protestants were almost equally balanced in numbers, and where there was fierce economic competition for land. Recent research suggests that this explanation is too simple. The traditional view was that the first Orangemen were drawn from the lowest levels of the peasantry, led and organized by the gentry and used by them (and ultimately by the government) as a counterpoise to the United Irishmen, who by 1795 were desperately striving to unite Catholic and Protestant in a common national and reformist cause. The Orange Society thus entered the history books as a conservative, sectarian and counter-revolutionary force brought into play by the genuine revolutionary movement of the United Irishmen. Marx so identified it, and it has been regarded as such by his followers. The same view is held by millions of Irish Catholics who are far from being Marxists, and by many Presbyterians who believe that none of their denomination was involved in its origins.

This last point is one of those on which the traditional thesis may be challenged. Earlier writers who stated that some of the lower order of Presbyterians in Armagh were members of the first lodges were thought to be in error, since the society was predominantly episcopalian, and for a long time Presbyterians would have nothing to do with it. Now it seems that they were right, and if this is true it poses an interesting question. Why did Presbyterians become United Irishmen in South Antrim but Orangemen in Armagh? Clearly the politics of Presbyterians depended more on local factors than on the ideological distinction between revolution and counter-revolution, between subversion and the authority of government.[20]

The factors involved seem indeed to be more complex than rivalry over land. For one thing, it is simply not true that the Armagh peasantry were the impoverished victims of chronic land hunger and a bad system of landholding. On the contrary, Armagh was so prosperous as a result of the linen industry that in 1804 it supported a population density of 429 people to the square mile on small farms which were not leased from middlemen. On the eve of the Famine it was the most densely populated county in Ireland, with 511 persons to the square mile. It is in this primitive industrial society that we must look for the origins of Orangeism. Those most deeply involved in the activities which brought it to birth were not landless peasants but the relatively secure weavers. The journeymen weavers were a notoriously independent element in rural society.[21]

It was in relation to this domestic industry that the balance of population became significant. If the province of Ulster is taken as a whole, the numbers of Catholics and Protestants are almost even, but this balance is reflected in very few localities. In Antrim and Down, for example, the Catholic population was concentrated, until the rapid expansion of Belfast, in two small areas outside the economy of the region. These posed no threat to Protestant domination of local industry. In Armagh, however, the two communities were equal in numbers. Recently it has been argued that the rapid progress of the linen industry upset the long-standing 'structured' inequalities between Catholic and Protestant, and so led the weavers to attack Catholics for breaking through the traditional 'limits' in the economic field.[22]

Once this aggression began, it followed the familiar patterns of the rural vendetta. Seasonal encounters at fairs, horse races and cock fights had long been a feature of rural life in many parts of

Ireland. The 'faction fights' were notorious in areas such as Limerick where there was no sectarian division in the populace, and at Donnybrook Fair, held outside Dublin each August, the fights were almost in the nature of a tourist attraction. 'Above the noise of buying and selling were heard the warwhoops, "Who dare say boo! who dare tread on the tail of me coat!" exclaimed by bands of men, or factions, dancing through the fair, trailing their coats in the mud behind them, shouting, yelling, screaming, and excitedly waving their sticks over their heads. When two rival parties met, they belaboured each other with might and main amid a terrific din of cries and exclamations, and the rattle of sticks in fierce collision.'[23]

Trailing one's coat was thus not a mere figure of speech. Such gestures as coat-trailing, stepping on the coat, and 'wheeling' (circling the opposition while calling out such provocative challenges as 'Who dare strike a Ryan?') were part of the preliminary rituals of provocation so characteristic of Irish confrontations. Faction fights, though often over slight and contrived quarrels, were serious encounters, and frequently led to bloody family or regional feuds. Clashes between the 'three-year-olds' and 'four-year-olds' in Co. Limerick went on for generations over a difference of opinion at some time in the remote past on the age of a cow. In Tipperary the feud between the Magpies and Black Hens caused sporadic outbreaks of violence well into the nineteenth century.[24]

This helps to explain why in origin the feuds of Co. Armagh were not sectarian at all. The factor which changed the character of these traditional brawls was the rise of the Volunteers between 1778 and 1784, a consequence of the effect on Ireland of the war with America. The Volunteer movement, out of which both the United Irishmen and the Orange Society were later to develop, gave a military character to the patterns of conflict, and this has persisted right up to the present. It is no coincidence that the serious trouble in Armagh began in 1784, for that was the year when the Volunteer movement lost political momentum and began to break up. In a desperate effort to strengthen its popular base, some Volunteer corps opened their ranks to the Catholics. Such a change inevitably caused ill-feeling in the evenly divided county of Armagh, which had been in the forefront of the early Volunteer organization. The year was also one of widespread unrest and disturbance throughout Ireland.

In these circumstances the question of Catholics possessing arms became a contentious one. The Penal Laws still prohibited Catholics from holding arms legally, but there was no agency capable of enforcing the law. The beginning of the prolonged sectarian war in Armagh has been traced to the intervention of a Catholic in a fight between two Presbyterians at the fair in Market-hill, shortly before the Belfast Volunteers presented an address to Lord Charlemont on 12 July 1784. The sequence of events was succinctly outlined by the Rev. Mortimer O'Sullivan in his evidence to the select committee of Parliament on Orange Lodges in 1835:

'The commencement of the system of Defenderism was apparently of a local and personal character rather than religious or political. At a fair in the north of Ireland, I think the fair of Port Norris, there was a pugilistic encounter between two individuals, both of them Presbyterians; a Roman Catholic was the second of one of these men, and, it was said, by some unfair assistance given by him to the person whom he seconded, the antagonist was overcome and severely beaten. In consequence there was a challenge given by the vanquished party to have a second encounter. They met at another fair, numbers crowded in on either side, and that which had been at first a duel became enlarged into a general fight. After various encounters and outrages, associations were formed of a parochial nature, parish against parish, and were called Fleets; the naval war was then in its pride. As yet there was no visible religious distinction; the associations formed were Presbyterians and Roman Catholics conjointly, but gradually one of these parties became subject a good deal to Roman Catholic influence, and religious or sectarian acrimony gave a new character to the factions. What I have stated is matter of history; I am about to add a circumstance which assisted much in creating divisions among the disturbers, and which, I believe, is simply traditional. The associations were, as I have already stated, called Fleets. At first they were distinguished by local denominations; one was the Bawn Fleet; one the Nappuck;* one, in which two districts were

* i.e. Nappagh

united, and which certainly was not exclusively Roman Catholic, called its members Defenders. Some alarm and suspicion appear to have been caused by a title given to one of these fleets, which consisted exclusively of Roman Catholics, it was the Brass Fleet. . . . It would appear that there was a great falling off of the numbers of the Presbyterian party, and that to prevent or allay suspicion the nomenclature of the Roman Catholic associations was changed, the name Brass Fleet was given up, and that of Defenders adopted. There appears to be considerable doubt whether they were the aggressors at the time when the mutual aggressions of Peep-of-day Boys and Defenders commenced. I never have been able to satisfy myself, but think it not impossible that the Peep-of-day Boys were incited to commence their aggressions at this early period, 1784, under the notion that they were enforcing the Popery laws.'[25]

A key source for the development of this strange war is *An impartial account of the late disturbances in the County of Armagh* by J. Byrne, a rare pamphlet published in Dublin in 1792. Byrne, who was probably the John Byrne who represented the Catholics of Armagh on the Catholic Committee, relates the chance beginnings of the quarrel and then proceeds to give a vivid circumstantial account of how the disturbances developed in 1785. Note the amazing familiarity of some of its aspects.

'This year the first company of Armagh volunteers published a manifesto against the Peep o'Day Boys for plundering the Papists of arms and concluded that there was a disgraceful zeal that seemed to have actuated both parties. This patriotic corps marched in conjunction with the artillery company to Lisnadill church. They all vowed to protect the Roman Catholics as far as in their power lay. The Peep o'Day Boys took umbrage at this menace and vowed vengeance against such of the Catholics as were Volunteers and swore that they would disarm them also. However, some of them got word and had they paid their intended visit on the appointed night, I do believe that some one of them would have got peppered legs. The family of the house which was threatened took proper steps to thwart these nocturnal heroes, for a great number of the inhabitants and volunteers of Armagh formed an ambush in the garden whilst another party were stationed in the house. A minister of the established church and a Popish priest were in the latter place as the family of this house were divided in religious sentiments, these gentlemen (no doubt) were to fight and pray alternately as occasion offered, for each party. However, the Peep o'Day Boys smelled a rat and stood aloof.

'Being disappointed on this night they were determined to make a trial in the town of Armagh. Accordingly a great number were posted in the market house whilst another party went to the house of a respectable Roman Catholic and rapped at the door of his house. The continual clamour they kept up for a considerable time awoke a worthy Protestant that lives next door to this gentleman's house. He gave them a severe reprimand and dismissed them from their nocturnal enterprise. They now vowed vengeance against this worthy man and set off to his tenant's house in the Wastelands on the road to Hamilton's Bawn, and forced open his door and carried off a gun that he lent his tenant to protect his property from the insults of these noctivagant gentry. Many protestant gentlemen lent arms to Papists at this period of the disturbances to protect themselves from the depredations of these fanatic madmen and many poor creatures were obliged to abandon their houses at night and sleep in turf bogs, in little huts made of sods, so great was the zeal of our holy crusaders this year.

'The neighbourhood of Granemore, near Ballymacanab, was tormented this year in a most shocking manner and many of the tenants of my Lord Charlemont came to the desperate resolution of giving up their leases and to retire to a foreign land. However they were advised by some gentlemen to purchase arms to defend themselves, but as fast as they got them they were taken from them until they came to the resolution of watching up at night in their respective turns. There were two desperate Peep o'Day captains in this neighbourhood that carried all before them. One of them was taken and tried this year and the most positive proofs brought home against him, but the mistaken lenity of the jury acquitted him and set him loose a second time. And were it not for this hero's acquittal I do believe the Granemore Defenders would have quit the thoughts of purchasing any more arms at this period, but seeing no protection from the law they formed companies of Defenders to protect their houses and were supplied with arms by a Protestant shopkeeper of the town of Armagh.

'A party of the Nappagh fleet paid a visit to the neighbourhood of Willisgrange, near Loughall, and entered the house of a poor man that never was able to purchase a gun in his life. They dragged his wife and five small children out of a straw bed and cut his web in the loom and destroyed what little provisions were in the house. For these nocturnal gentry could not subsist, for being mostly journeymen weavers, they could not work in the daytime after wanting their rest at night and of course must live by plundering their neighbours. The poor woman of the house (unfortunately for herself and family) was pregnant; the rough handling she received from these gallant heroes occasioned her premature death the day after.'[26]

Thus while in Belfast some of the original Volunteers eventually became United Irishmen, disposed to unite with Catholics in the cause of reform and Catholic emancipation, in Armagh the Volunteers maintained the ancient attitudes. One Sunday morning in November 1788, for example, the Benburb Volunteers paraded in uniform and side-arms in order to march to church in Armagh. 'They had proceeded about two miles when there appeared on the road and in the neighbourhood an unusual number of people, who they supposed had assembled to see them pass. One of the Volunteers, who was prevented from attending on parade, intended following, and his bayonet and belt were given to a boy who was walking with the party. At the part of the road I have mentioned one of the crowd snatched the bayonet from the boy, and ran off with it across the fields; a number of the Volunteers ran after, when he dropped the bayonet and took to a house. They attempted to follow, but a musquet was presented at them, and they were immediately attacked with stones by the crowd, which obliged them to seek their safety in flight, some of them being cut and bruised by the stones thrown at them. After service, Mr Young, having received certain information that they would be way-laid on their return, he and such of the party as had acquaintances in town borrowed arms (in all eleven stand) to take with them, either to intimidate the party by their appearance or defend themselves if attacked. On reaching the place where the scuffle happened in the morning, they saw several hundred men assembled at a narrow, hollow part of the road, where they had collected heaps of stones which they intended to make use of in their attack. Mr. Young sent forward some of the countrymen he saw on the road to intreat they would not attempt to interrupt the Volunteers in getting home, and to assure them he had no intention whatever to molest them. A message was sent him that they might pass unmolested, on which they went forward and had almost got through the crowd (which lined the ditches on each side of the road), when a few stones were first thrown, and instantly after a volley from all quarters, which knocked down two or three Volunteers and struck many more. Mr. Staples (who had not a musquet) being one of those knocked down, cried: "D—n you, fire, or we'll be all murdered!" on which three or four of the party fired, which not taking effect, the assailants cried: "D—n them, they have nothing but powder!" and continued stoning them. A second party instantly fired, and two who were foremost in the attack were wounded and fell. Mr. Young ordered the Volunteers to quit the road, or they would be surrounded, on which they crossed into a field, and he, in attempting to follow, was knocked down by a stone, and when down his piece was taken from him. The crowd that attempted striking him was so great that they prevented others from doing him material injury, till two or three of them who knew him were actuated by humanity and declared he should not be farther injured, but dragged him out of the ditch and got him from among the crowd. On Mr. Young's being knocked down a number of shot were fired, and a sort of running fight continued in which three or four more men were wounded. The Volunteers halted at some distance till Mr. Young was brought to them. One of the first two that were wounded died in a few minutes. The other received a ball in his knee, which went out at his hip and broke the thighbone, but [he] is in a fair way of recovery, as are the others, who I understand were wounded but slightly.'[27]

This unhappy encounter produced predictable consequences. At the inquest on the man who died, Catholic witnesses declared that they had assembled with an intention to disarm and beat the Volunteers, but that they had no intention of killing any of them. The reason for the attack was that the Volunteers had played tunes insulting to Catholics, namely 'The Protestant Boys' and the

'Boyne Water'. The funeral was attended by 'immense multitudes' of Catholics from many miles around, and Protestants feared that some attempt at retaliation might take place. The use of the funeral of a victim as a form of popular protest is incidentally very characteristic of this tradition, and it persists today.

In December another of the wounded Defenders died, and a magistrate took depositions from Catholic witnesses who now alleged that they had gone unarmed to watch the Volunteers and had been fired upon without provocation. A warrant was issued against two of the Volunteers, but before it could be executed some hundreds of Defenders, most of them armed with firelocks, and the rest with swords and spears, assembled about the bleach-house and green of Messrs. Jackson and Eyre, near Benburb, in order to apprehend the two Volunteers, who worked there as bleachers. The threatened men secured themselves in the mill with arms, and withstood a siege all that night and the following day, until the army arrived from Armagh barracks. They then surrendered to the soldiers and were taken to Armagh where they were placed on bail for their appearance at the next assize.

This kind of rural vendetta sets the model for the many encounters between Orangemen and Catholics after the founding of the Orange Society in 1795. The 'Battle of the Diamond', or 'Running Monday', which led to the formation of the first lodges was itself one of these affrays, and there were earlier examples, such as that at Lisnagade in 1791. Of those which took place in the nineteenth century perhaps the most notorious was the one which occurred at Dolly's Brae, near Castlewellan in Co. Down in 1847, when Ribbonmen confronted the Orangemen on their way both to and from the estate of the Earl of Roden at Tollymore. On the return a lighted squib was thrown into the procession, and in the resulting exchange of fire six Catholics were killed.

The Orange Order cannot, of course, be considered simply as yet another of the agrarian secret armies. From a very early stage it exerted influence at two levels of Ulster society, for some elements of the Armagh gentry assumed the leadership of the movement, and this proved to be very opportune on the eve of the 1798 insurrection. The suggestion has always been made that the Irish administration in the last years of the century deliberately fomented the quarrels between Protestant and Catholic in a classic demonstration of the policy of 'divide and rule'. There is actually very little evidence that this was so, and some evidence that the official attitude was quite the reverse.

For example, Lord Gosford, who was appointed governor of Co. Armagh in 1791 in succession to the Volunteer leader Lord Charlemont, was strenuously opposed to the Orange Society. In December 1795 he called a meeting of Co. Armagh landowners to condemn the persecution of the Catholics, although on 12 July he had permitted the Orangemen to parade through his demesne at Markethill—an attempt perhaps to strengthen the hand of the Orange leaders in controlling the rank and file. The government was in fact reluctant to allow the organization of 'loyal associations', but it became concerned that the militia included large numbers of United Irishmen, and so decided to establish the yeomanry which rapidly became Orange. There were frequent and bloody clashes between the militia and yeomanry between 1795 and 1798, and this conflict was central to the fighting in Ulster during the rebellion itself.

The conflict in Co. Armagh passed on two traditions to the wider Orange movement of the nineteenth century and after. The rural labourers and the new urban working class created by Belfast's linen mills and shipyards inherited the Peep o'Day Boys' militant anti-Catholicism and their rituals of confrontation. The Armagh gentry of the Established Church were succeeded over the years by the Ulster landed classes, the clergy and the politicians, for whom the Order provided a loyal vassalage, an electorate and ultimately a citizen army.

# 4. The Black City

At the height of the Ulster crisis of 1914, when nearly one hundred thousand northern Protestants were enrolled in the Ulster Volunteer Force and pledged to resist home rule by every means within their power, the newspapers frequently carried the headline WILL ULSTER FIGHT? It meant, of course, 'Will Ulster

Protestants fight the British army in order to remain within the United Kingdom?' In a book published that year the journalist F. Frankfort Moore pointed out that the newspapers had been carrying that headline from the time of his earliest recollections fifty years before, and that it bore little relevance to the real fight which was still going on in Ulster after three centuries. The question was the wrong one: it ought to have been WILL ULSTER STOP FIGHTING?

In its nineteenth-century manifestation the Ulster struggle impinged on English consciousness chiefly in the disagreeable form of Belfast riots, providing a headline which 'recurred as faithfully as Halley's comet or the eruption of Mount Vesuvius'.[28] This phenomenon of periodic rioting was unknown in Britain. The Chartists of the 1840s, the socialist rioters who pulled down the Hyde Park railings in the 1880s, and the followers of John Burns who twenty years later fought with the Guards in Trafalgar Square, did not fit into a sinister pattern of recurrent violence. In Belfast, however, riots were a fact of life.

Though serious riots, including sectarian riots, have occurred from time to time in Britain, it was no doubt because of the sheer unfamiliarity of the spectacle that British people, watching the savage street fighting of 1969 on television, exhibited such appalled reactions, and jumped to erroneous conclusions about the nature of what was happening. For example, it would have occurred to very few of them that thousands of people in Belfast who had never seen a riot were watching the same scenes on their television sets with identical sensations of horror and curiosity.

The inability of English people in particular to comprehend either the ground or the essential character of the troubles derived partly from the peculiar insularity of English experience in this respect. As Dr. George Steiner wrote in 1973: 'There is no English analogue to the Albigensian crusade, to the massacre of St. Bartholomew, to the long rule of the Inquisition, to the devastating fanaticism of the Thirty Years' War. There is hardly a European city which does not bear traces of scission and apartheid as between doctrinal communities. The present ugliness in Northern Ireland, with which English sentiment is finding it so difficult to cope, represents an atavistic but also routine aspect of Continental history. So much of Europe is a consequence of exhaustion after generations of religious civil warfare. Dogmatic fury has played a minor, sporadic role in the English scene.'[29]

Even the minor episodes of dogmatic fury do not lie as far back in English history as might be imagined. The Gordon riots of 1780 were by no means the last sectarian riots in Britain. In 1852, for example, during riots in Stockport, Lancashire, the Irish were driven back into their own quarter of the town, two Catholic chapels were wrecked, and in one of them the tabernacle was broken open, and the sacred hosts spilt on the ground.[30]

Nevertheless in 1969 there was a widespread feeling that the situation in Northern Ireland was an alien and un-British one, and that the army was being called upon to undertake some entirely novel and un-British role. This was far from the case. A century ago the British army was deployed in the streets of Belfast, being jeered at, stoned and fired on, under strict orders not to fire back, and in a state of total incomprehension about the nature of the quarrel it was called on to stop. Here is a description of the Lady Day riots of 15 August 1872 taken from the *Illustrated London News*.

'In the evening of the next day, the two parties met for a pitched battle, to the number of several thousands, in the brick-fields between the Shankill and Falls Roads. The police tried in vain to separate them and the military were sent for: sixty men of the 4th Royal Dragoons, and a detachment of the 78th Highlanders, forced the combatant mobs apart but showers of stones were thrown over the heads of the line of soldiery, and fierce howls of mutual execration were exchanged by hostile bands of Irishmen, who were prevented from slaughtering each other.

'The houses ... on the Shankill Road and in adjoining streets have been gutted by mobs who took the furniture out and burnt it in the street. ... It was pitiable to see the families leaving their houses as though going into captivity or exile, and hear the lamentations of the women and children. Protestants living in Roman Catholic districts and Catholics living in Protestant districts have found it necessary to change their quarters and go to their respective friends for protection.'[31]

This report hardly differs in any particular from those which appeared in the English press in the 1970s, or for that matter in the 1920s. In his book Moore illustrates this in a vivid way. As it happened, a Belfast riot was one of his first childhood memories. One Sunday afternoon his nurse, a Presbyterian with 'connections in the mercantile marine', had taken him without his parents' knowledge on a visit to her relatives in the dockside area of Belfast, where from a bedroom window he had witnessed 'a flying crowd of men and women, boys and girls of the mill-working order, and behind them ... riding at the trot three dragoons with their sabres drawn and at the "carry" '.

Later that evening, when the streets had been cleared and quietened, the nurse set off on the hazardous route towards the safety of home. Rounding a corner they came upon a white-haired elderly gentleman on horseback, with dragoons on either side of him and a whole line of soldiers with rifles and bayonets fixed. 'The old gentleman removed his hat as if he recognised a lady at a distance, and then began to read, very badly indeed, something from a paper which he tried to hold in a suitable position before his eyes. ... After a very poor display of elocution, and a deplorable one of horsemanship, we heard the words "God Save the Queen", followed by a hoarse "Present arms!" from a mounted officer wearing a shako with a little white ball poised at the top in front; while he gave his sword a twist and brought the hilt up to his face, and then lowered the point of the blade. There was a clash of rifles all down the line of red-coated infantry.'[32] This description is all the more effective because of the contrast between the Quality Street uniforms of the troops and the entire familiarity of what they were doing. The riots were probably those of 1857— the year of the Indian Mutiny—and they were by no means a new phenomenon in Belfast.

The first of these Belfast sectarian riots took place as early as 1812, and it is clear that it marked the transfer to the urban environment of well-established patterns of violence. Further outbreaks occurred in 1835, 1841, 1843, and 1852. In 1857 riots on a larger scale and of more serious character laid the foundations of Belfast's baleful reputation, for this form of major eruption recurred periodically throughout the rest of the century, in 1864, 1872 and 1886, with lesser disorders in 1880, 1884 and 1898. The riots of 1886 were so serious as to assume the character of civil war. Minor outbreaks occurred in the early twentieth century (in 1907, 1909 and 1912) but the rioting which merged in the Anglo-Irish troubles of 1919–21, continued through 1922 (the worst year), and ended only with the outbreak of the civil war in southern Ireland, produced more casualties than all the nineteenth-century riots taken together. The only bad riots to occur during the fifty years of Unionist government erupted in 1935, and after that year there were no riots at all in Belfast until the Divis Street riots of 1964, and the terrible aftermath of the political events of 1969. The pattern of riots in Londonderry since 1800 has been roughly, but not exactly, coincident with that of Belfast: the worst outbreaks occurred in 1869 and 1883.

For some reason, this sombre but dramatic and fascinating pattern of violence prompted little serious investigation by historians until the romanticization of the urban guerrilla in other countries made the subject fashionable.[33] In recent years, with the return of serious civil disturbance in Northern Ireland, it has attracted attention from social scientists of various kinds interested in 'conflict theory'. It is very doubtful whether the history of Belfast urban warfare throws much light on similar conflict elsewhere but a more scientific approach to the evidence has yielded results of considerable interest, and many ingenious theories have been advanced to elucidate the actual mechanics of mob activity. Inevitably, too, some of this earnest investigation has simply created new terms for old problems, substituting 'ethnic slums' and 'shatter zones' for matters of common observation and common sense. One has always to remember that facts well enough known to every Belfast street urchin have to be translated into learned jargon for university professors abroad.

Outside Ulster, two widely accepted but erroneous assumptions were made about civil disturbance and they remained the basis for most discussion of it. One was that the two communities were totally at war with each other, and in every part of the province. The other was that such behaviour was mindless, indiscriminate and undisciplined: words like 'primitive', 'tribal', 'barbaric', were used to describe it, not in their true sense, but simply in order to express revulsion, and to distinguish it from a superior form of civilized life which was deemed to exist elsewhere. In the long run, and quite inevitably once the process was allowed to develop, it became no longer possible to maintain this fiction, which only revealed that men in an ordered society quite deliberately deceive themselves about the subject of human nature, wisely perhaps, since such illusions are essential to its health.

The conflict was not total, of course, either in numbers or in area. On the contrary, only a very small fraction of the entire population was involved in violence of any kind. We must, however, make a distinction between two aspects of violence; one consists of the war between the I.R.A. and the security forces, the other of the war between the two communities. The first could only occur when the second had developed, as infection will develop in a wound. Behind the bombing campaign and the gunning down of police and troops there lies a far older sectarian war. It keeps the urban guerrilla in business, yet paradoxically in the long run it cheats him of even the faintest possibility of success. His only hope of eventual revolutionary victory is in communities where nine-tenths of the population are either on his side or at least not hostile to him.

Moreover, in this context we are concerned only with the specialized form of violence which is manifested in city riots. Severe riots occurred, in the traditional pattern, in the early stages of the Ulster troubles. They ceased, as they ceased in earlier troubles, once the use of firearms became widespread. For the disorders follow a predictable pattern, like the course of a disease; yet it is hardly recognized outside Ulster that during the long years of the troubles the character of violence has changed every month. What was happening in Belfast in 1977 was very different from what was happening there in 1969.

# 5. Seismic Zones

All these aspects were shrewdly noted by Moore some sixty years ago. Ulster was then, and is still, politically a volcanic region, 'one of those volcanic basins which only need a single stone to be flung into them to produce such an eruption as may change the whole face of the landscape'.[34] It is so because the molten lava of political and religious passion lies only a short distance below its tranquil earth. All this is obvious enough, but what is less appreciated is that the cracks and weak places in the earth where the lava will break through are always the same, and can be plotted accurately on the map. Moore noticed that Belfast had well-defined 'seismic' zones, and this is still true today. Once again, topography is all-important to the understanding of events.

These seismic areas were created by Belfast's phenomenal expansion in the first half of the nineteenth century. In 1791 Belfast was still a small market town with a harbour, but by 1825 it had already assumed its present status as an industrial city and port. As it grew, its relation to Ulster, and to Ireland, changed, and its economy became more closely linked with that of Great Britain. Although the Union was blamed for retarding the industrial development of the rest of Ireland, it brought prosperity to Belfast and the fertile Lagan Valley in which it was situated.

At the end of the eighteenth century the population of Belfast was predominantly Presbyterian, but because the dissenters were legally debarred from sitting on corporations, the borough was controlled by the nominees of the Chichester family. The proportion of Catholics living in Belfast was very small, less than 5 per cent, and this was one reason why the Presbyterians of Belfast after 1780 became enthusiastic in the cause of toleration. The politics of Presbyterians in Armagh or Cavan were, as we have seen, of a very different cast. The first Catholic church, St. Mary's in Chapel Lane, was built in 1784. On 30 May in that year the (Protestant) Volunteers marched to the church and formed a guard of honour for the parish priest, the Rev. Hugh O'Donnell, when he arrived to celebrate Mass for the first time. They generously subscribed to the building fund, and the vicar of Belfast, the Rev. William Bristow, paid for the new pulpit out of his own pocket. The ecumenical spirit, of which this was the most celebrated example, briefly survived the 1798 insurrection. Lord Donegall leased to Father O'Donnell a site in Upper Donegall Street for a second church, St. Patrick's, and gave a piece of land at Friar's Bush, near Stranmillis, for a Catholic burying ground.[35]

During the first half of the nineteenth century this cordiality between Protestant and Catholic in Belfast rapidly disappeared. One widely accepted explanation of this is that it was the consequence of 'the rise of the bigots', the triumph of the reactionary elements in the Presbyterian community over the liberal, and the spread of the Orange Order among the episcopalians.[36] But this is to mistake the consequence for the cause. The real reason for the increasing hostility was the rapid increase in the Catholic population. The remarkably swift industrialization of Belfast after 1800 drastically altered the plantation mosaic of settlement in eastern Ulster, by drawing into Belfast vast numbers of workers, not only from the hinterland, but from Catholic areas in the west and south. By the mid-century the Catholic proportion of the population was 35 per cent, and after the Famine the process was greatly accelerated until the present position was reached, that the Catholic proportion of the population in the city is much greater than for eastern Ulster generally.

Most of the Catholics who came into Belfast settled along the line of the Falls Road leading into the city from the west, so that the main area of Catholic settlement ultimately formed a large irregular wedge between two extensive Protestant working-class sectors about the Shankill Road and Sandy Row. The apex of this wedge reaches the city centre at Castle Street, near to St. Mary's Church. Old maps show that this was formerly Mill Street, which was situated just outside the old town walls of the seventeenth century, the nearest point at which the mistrusted 'Irish' were permitted to form permanent homes. Two smaller concentrations of Catholic population, lying to the north and south of the city centre, may each have grown from a similar nucleus of Catholic population at the town walls. A third grew up in the north of the city at Ardoyne, and a fourth, the most isolated and vulnerable, is situated across the river in East Belfast, with its focus St. Matthew's Catholic Church.[37]

The segregation of these zones, which seems so abnormal to the outsider, arises not from these origins but from the effects of subsequent riots during the nineteenth and twentieth centuries. The pattern set in the seventeenth and eighteenth centuries has thus hardly changed since. The prospect of change, indeed, is itself a potent cause of renewed rioting. To say that the modern conflict in Ireland is dictated by the topography of seventeenth-century walled towns may seem absurd to city dwellers for whom city gates are now only the names of Underground stations. Nevertheless, it is perfectly true. Moreover the behaviour of people on these frontiers is perfectly rational, not only in terms of history but of contemporary politics; it is not the mark of too much or too little Christianity, or any kind of attitude not found in the rest of the human race.

# 6. Sermons in Stones

No one who has been caught in a Belfast riot against his will is likely to regard it as one of the higher forms of human activity, which is one reason why most of the population of Belfast prefer to watch riots on television. It can only be assumed that feelings of intense hatred, combined with the excitement of participation, somehow anaesthetize the individual rioter to its horror and its dangers, often with fatal consequences. But it is a naïve and fundamental error to regard rioting as a 'mindless' and irrational mode of human behaviour. Stone-throwing, for example, is a military art of considerable sophistication and great antiquity.[38] Even in the twentieth century, well-organized stone-throwing can inflict very serious casualties on armed and disciplined troops who are forbidden to shoot the stone-throwers. That simple fact has determined the image of Ulster most frequently presented to the world—that of well-armed soldiers and police cowering behind armoured cars and street corners under a hail of bricks and stones. These soldiers might as well be Roman legionaries, for all the good their modern weapons are; their only protection is a shield, a steel helmet and a visor. Schoolboys can dance right up to the armoured vehicles and launch a brick or a nail-bomb with deadly accuracy, but woe to the soldier who fires a single round, with or without orders; not the least of the rioters' advantages is in the field of propaganda. The stone-throwers may be barbarians, savages, Neanderthal men, but from a military point of view, they know what they are doing. Their art has been perfected in the streets of Belfast and Derry, Lurgan and Portadown, for a century and a half at least.

A proper appreciation of this caused the paving of Belfast in the early nineteenth century to be a matter of great concern to the city fathers. Many of the city's streets and squares were originally paved with cobble stones, which were found in quantities along the coasts of Antrim and Down. These, from their shape, were known locally as 'kidney stones', and were a highly prized and readily available source of ammunition. When macadamized surfaces of broken granite and basalt were introduced, they proved even more useful to rioters. The scene which Frankfort Moore witnessed as a child was enacted in the streets round the Custom House, in the Belfast dockland. This building, or, more accurately, the flight of steps in front of it, was traditionally Belfast's equivalent of Speakers' Corner, and on Sunday afternoons it frequently became a pulpit, from which 'highly-seasoned Protestant doctrines' were preached. This open-air preaching was sometimes, as in 1857, the actual cause of the riots; and since the square where Victoria Street, High Street and Corporation Street met had a loose macadam surface, the whole neighbourhood would, after 'a warm interchange of opinion on the basis of basalt', assume the appearance of a battlefield, and 'the strain upon the resources of the surgical staff of the hospital' would reach breaking point.[39]

The corporation therefore decided to substitute 'a more prehensile system of paving in all the argumentative localities of the town'. Heavy granite squares, called 'setts', were put down instead. They did not bring peace, but, as Moore observes, 'there was a marked difference in the range at which the discussion began'.[40]

Further experiments were made, and ultimately all new streets were paved with flagstones, though this placed a heavy burden on the ratepayers. Even this did not stop the habit, for the flagstones were pulled up by rioters and broken into smaller pieces.

The stoning was not carried out in a haphazard way. Moore describes how he learned 'the proper way to conduct a street riot' in Portadown in 1869. 'Every boy and girl in the crowd understood the art thoroughly. When the police charged in military fashion, they hurried to one side or the other, refraining from obstructing them in the least, but returning immediately afterward to the place they had occupied before the "charge".'[41] The reminiscences of the architect Robert Young, a distinguished Belfast citizen who died in 1917, make the same point:

'This was my first experience of rioting. I mean I was so near the stonethrowers that I saw the women gathering stones in their aprons and supplying their male friends with this ammunition. . . .

'In the shameful riots lately that culminated in the loss of two or probably more lives these kidney pavers played a leading part. Judging by the accounts of the police and military they were prepared beforehand in a systematic plan for the assault of the military *in the ordinary way* [my italics] and also by flinging pavers over the spaces between the narrow streets jutting from the Falls Road where it was expected their enemies must pass. Stores of these pavers were prepared in the upper rooms of the workers' houses, and when the riotous mob was being driven through one of these streets up came the windows and an avalanche of paving stones descended on the heads of the ill-fated Tommies. It was the outcome of a most carefully planned and almost accomplished scheme for massacring the English soldiers that had been brought to the city on account of the incipient mutiny of the constabulary. Law and order were vindicated, but not till many wounded had been carried to the hospitals.'[42]

In the very serious riots of 1886 Moore observed all these tactics in use again. He had in the meantime seen nasty riots elsewhere in the world, but in his opinion none of the principals in these actions knew anything of strategy when 'compared with those who engineered the sacking of York Street on a dark night in August 1886'.

'The lamps had nearly all been extinguished—perhaps they had not been lighted at all—but when I came to the mouth of the road, scarcely a light was to be seen; still I had no difficulty in making out the movements of the dense crowds surging in every direction, and shot after shot I heard above the shouts that suggested something very like Pandemonium. Once or twice I was carried along in the rush of people before a police charge, and I was taught in the most practical way how to avoid a casualty; for I was simply hurried through the street and into the nearest by-lane, where I was forced to stand with the rest of the fugitives until the projectile, in the form of a squad of police or soldiers, had charged past. Then I was allowed a leisurely return to the field of battle. . . . I felt I had learned something of the impotence of every arm except artillery in the case of street fighting.'[43]

Gradually it becomes clear that these periodical outbursts of violence follow a complex internal logic of their own, which is un-altered by the current political circumstances, the ululation of politicians and clergy, or the military strength used to suppress it. The 'troubles' (to use the Irish term which is more comprehensive than rioting) go through well-defined stages. The first is usually confined to provocation of the opposite party, intense and often prolonged over weeks and months. This provocation, which is not the cause of the ultimate outbreak, but appears to be a ritual part of it, may take the form of marching, jeering, waving flags and singing party songs. Where a main road divides Catholic streets from Protestant the displaying of flags and hurling of insults may go on all through the summer, slowly building up to the inevitable clashes and bloodshed. The first stage is followed by physical violence, fisticuffs, stone-throwing, forays into enemy territory by men armed with clubs, the smashing of windows and the starting of fires. This automatically introduces the police who must take the routine steps to preserve the peace, apprehend trouble-makers and, if possible, separate the two mobs. The violence is then re-directed by one side or the other towards the police, who are accused either of partiality or over-reaction. It is not unusual for both sides to attack the police, or for one side to cease hostilities in order to enjoy the spectacle of the other fighting it out with the police.

The police begin to sustain casualties; reinforcements are called in, and the conflict is aggravated. If really serious disorders develop, the police will lose control of the situation and be obliged to call for military aid. At some point before this stage is reached, the whole character of this ritual dance of provocation and aggression will have been changed by the use of firearms. The firing of weapons at night, from a quarter which is predominantly of one religion, may often be simply a signal to the other side that the inhabitants mean business; but it usually begins unexpectedly and dramatically when someone emerges from a jeering crowd and deliberately fires a weapon into the opposing crowd. The reaction is total shock, and bitter recrimination, conducted on the basis that no one in the long history of Ireland has ever seen a gun, let alone used one, and that the other side have broken the rules, in the most treacherous manner, which is all one can expect from them.

The first use of firearms is always by the other side, and there is invariably a sensation of shock and anger at the elevation of the conflict to a more lethal plane. This creates a momentary pause, followed by indiscriminate retaliation. Death and injury initiate the vendetta, and if it has been caused by police or troops, then they are fired on also. Actual contests between Protestant and Catholic mobs do not last long. Some of the worst, like the 'Battle of the Brickfields' in 1872, have been over in twenty minutes, but sporadic rioting, cowardly assassination and attacks on the police and troops may continue for days or weeks. A 'flashpoint' usually cools in three or four days. The rioters seem to tire of the activity, no doubt because of extreme physical exhaustion, and the rioting may be transferred to another locality, where the able-bodied men are fresh for combat. Riots die away for no apparent reason, or for reasons which seem illogical; for example the prolonged fighting of 1886 ended because of three days of continuous rain. That is to say, the rioters were more demoralized by rain than by rifle fire.

Moore shrewdly noticed an aspect of rioting which is just as apparent today as it was a century ago. The army is almost totally ineffective as a means of restoring order. It would of course be extremely effective if it were allowed to operate *as an army*, but this is what it must never do. The addition of armed troops to the situation in the streets aggravates the disorders, and for the last one hundred and fifty years has been a required element in the scenario. If 'the military' did not take part, some essential ingredient in the street fighting would be felt to be absent. On the ineffectiveness of the army in 1886, Moore makes this significant comment. 'I have seen how little value troops are to put down a disturbance in a few streets of a large city even when every respectable inhabitant is hostile to the disturbers of the peace, and I have, I trust, sufficient imagination to know what would happen when every respectable person has gone over to the other side.'[44]

The Belfast riots of 1857, 1864 and 1886, and the Londonderry riots of 1869 and 1883, were the subject of commissions of inquiry. The evidence which they collected, and the reports which they finally presented, provide the historian with a vast amount of information on the peculiarities of this kind of urban warfare. After each riot the commissioners did their best to isolate what they believed to be the immediate and long-term causes, so that their labours might help to avert such events in future. The subsequent explosions clearly proved that they had not succeeded, and it may be assumed that the same is true of those commissions which have sat in recent years. With depressing frequency, the nineteenth-century commissions laid the blame squarely on two main factors —the partiality and inefficiency of the police, and the provocative nature of the Orange celebrations.

In 1857 the commissioners found that the town police of Belfast, a local force established by Act of Parliament in 1845 and separate from the Irish Constabulary, consisted of one hundred and sixty men, unarmed except for light walking sticks. Of these all but six or seven were Protestants 'and many were Orangemen'. They were considered sympathetic to the Sandy Row mob and enemies to the Catholic Pound; consequently they could appear safely in Sandy Row but not in the Pound. The police were attacked and had to be defended by the Constabulary. 'All these matters lead us to believe', the commissioners reported, 'that in the constitution of the present police force there are serious errors, calling for immediate remedy; and to recommend that a total change should be made in the mode of appointment and the management of the local police of Belfast.'[45]

In 1864 the commissioners alleged discrimination by Protestants in recruitment to the police. The town police force still numbered one hundred and sixty, but now there were only five Catholics. 'As regards the local police, the absolute necessity for change is universally acknowledged.'[46] By an Act of Parliament passed in 1865 the town police force was disbanded and the policing of the town was entrusted to the Irish Constabulary.

The formula of tinkering with the police was tried after each successive outbreak, and always without the slightest effect. The Irish Constabulary, the Royal Irish Constabulary and the Royal Ulster Constabulary were each in turn criticized for allowing riots to develop, and failing to contain them when they did develop. If they were unarmed, it was recommended that they should be armed; if they used their arms, it was recommended that they be disarmed. When Lord Hunt recommended in 1969 that the R.U.C. be instantly disarmed, he was, whether he knew it or not, following a well-established precedent. Again the move did not have the desired effects. On the contrary, it loosed a deluge of violence which led to the deaths of many policemen and soldiers, and hundreds of civilians. The police were quickly re-armed, but the damage had already been done—less from the disarming than from the general doubt cast upon the effectiveness and impartiality of the R.U.C. It was an old story, as the nineteenth-century riot reports show, and it had little to do with the I.R.A.

The commissioners found little difficulty in isolating what they believed to be the chief cause of riots in Belfast. They blamed the Orange lodges for the provocative displays which inflamed the atmosphere in Belfast during the weeks leading up to the Orange festival on 12 July. 'The celebration of that festival', declared the commissioners on the riot of 1857, 'is plainly and unmistakably the originating cause of these riots.' It was used 'to remind one party of the triumph of their ancestors over those of the other, and to inculcate the feelings of Protestant superiority over their Roman Catholic neighbours'.[47] This view has been accepted uncritically by many writers, and is heartily endorsed in the south of Ireland, while opinion outside Ireland often seeks no further explanation. In its crudest form it is used to explain the mechanism by which religious rancour is carried 'like a hereditary disease'[48] from generation to generation.

Such an explanation is probably too simple. A quarrel of this vitality cannot be sustained through the ages by provocations from one side only, and the strength of Orangeism depends upon opposite and equal forces of anti-Protestant feeling, often more subtly displayed. Again, the antithesis between the liberality of Belfast in the last decade of the eighteenth century and the intolerance of the years after 1830 is a false one, based on a misreading of the earlier period, and ignoring (among many other factors) the alteration in the balance of population caused by industrialization, which both sharpened the hostility and shaped the forms which it assumed.

One historian has calculated that Orange processions were 'a precipitating factor' in at least six out of fifteen major riots in Belfast between 1813 and 1914;[49] that is to say, they cannot be proved to be the cause of more than six out of the fifteen riots. Such a finding is not surprising, for there is a good deal more to the process of causing a riot than is apparent on the surface. The fact that an Orange procession is not the immediate cause of a riot does not exculpate the Orangemen from responsibility in helping to bring it about. To understand why requires some familiarity with the curious patterns of Belfast rioting. Orangemen, when engaged in their rituals, do not physically attack anyone, unless they are provoked beyond discipline. The provocation alleged by Catholics may arise simply from the fact that Orangeism is a symbol of something intensely hated; or from the display of party colours and playing of party tunes; or from that most menacing of sounds, even to Protestant ears, the thunder of Orange drums; or—the classic and strongest cause—from the routing of a procession through territory traditionally considered to be Catholic. Belfast riots have rarely, if ever, been begun by Orangemen marching in their regalia. The archetypal situation is for an Orange procession to be attacked by Catholics, so initiating full-scale retaliation at a time when 'Orange blood is up'.

The actual cause of an outbreak of rioting is not in any event the matter of first importance; it may be almost anything if the political atmosphere is ripe—the waving of a flag, a ranting sermon, a funeral, a Sunday school procession. 'To such an extent does the inflammability of the populace seem to extend,' reported the 1886 commission, 'that even the excursion through the town of school children ... if accompanied by a band, appears effectually to lead to an attack by the excursionists or the mobs who collect on hearing a band.'[50] The Orange summer revels would appear to be the most visible and colourful part of a much more complex, and largely concealed, structure of ritual social behaviour which has not yet been satisfactorily explained.

Terrorism in the advancement of a political cause is at once part of, and a new pattern imposed upon, the tapestry of civil disorder. It first appeared in its familiar modern form during the troubles of 1919–23, but it is probably a mistake to distinguish too sharply between traditional violence and that motivated by contemporary politics. The distinction lies in the use of more deadly weapons; the bomb and machine-gun have been added to the pistol and the pike. The troubles in Ireland after 1918 reflected both the technology and the horror of the First World War, and in turn set a pattern for nationalist terrorism throughout the world. In the north, the worst outrages followed the setting up of the State of Northern Ireland in 1920. Between June 1920 and June 1922 the total casualties were 428 killed and 1,766 wounded, a staggering increase on the remarkably low figures for persons killed in all the Belfast riots of the nineteenth century. The total deaths between 1813 and 1907 numbered 68, and of these almost half occurred in 1886.[51] At the time of writing the casualty figures for Northern Ireland since 1969 are approaching a total of 1,700 dead.

In both the earlier and the present campaigns, the original attacks by the I.R.A. provoked severe reprisals on the Catholic population. Once this mechanism is operated, it cannot be halted or reversed, except perhaps by resolute action by a popularly based administration which has the confidence of the Protestant majority. Thus a ceasefire declared by the I.R.A. has little effect on continuing sectarian violence. The whole process of muted insurrection, so familiar in Irish history, is an elaborately structured and ever-changing development which obeys no laws except those intrinsic to it. Once the civil rights movement assumed a militant, and to all intents and purposes a sectarian, form in 1969, the entire escalation of the conflict was easily predictable. This process has little to do with the merits of the civil rights issue as such.

The Ulster war has shown yet again that, irrespective of the political aims of those who resort to violence, the conflict has developed along lines determined by the cumulative experience of earlier clashes. When we turn to the nineteenth-century riot reports we find some of the familiar features of today: the setting up of barricades in Protestant areas of Belfast, the extinction of street lighting, the manufacture of home-made pistols and ammunition, the accusation that the police joined the Protestant rioters, the use of 'snatch squads' by the army to drag ringleaders from the mob, police complaints at meeting 'a wall of silence'. In 1864 and 1872 Catholic gun clubs were formed, and a Protestant Defence Association came into being. In 1872 the army was caught in the middle while trying to establish a peace line between the Falls and the Shankill; there was widespread burning, looting and intimidation in the streets between the two roads, which was precisely re-enacted in 1969 in the very same streets. In 1886 what are now called 'no-go areas' appeared after the police had been driven from the Shankill Road; after nearly two months, during which there was little ordinary crime, and the men of the area did their own vigilante policing, authority cautiously returned in the form of joint army–police patrols.

# PART FIVE

## Modes of Minority

# 1. 'A Partition of Sects'

Whatever the 'Ulster Question' is in Irish history, it is not the question of partition, though it is commonly presented as such throughout the world. The assumption that partition is the root of all Northern Ireland's ills dominates discussion of the problem but does not much illuminate it. On the contrary, it inhibits thought, and throws into darkness the complicated texture of the problem itself. Not much thought is required to perceive that the evidence of history points rather to an opposite conclusion, that partition is more a symptom of the problem than its cause. (It may of course exacerbate the problem, but that is another matter.) The problem is clearly older than partition and would in all probability survive it. Thus if one could imagine the border abolished over-night, and a government in Dublin assuming responsibility for the whole country, far from being settled, as so many Irishmen believe, the Ulster problem would become acute.

After all, partition is not peculiar to Ireland, though Irishmen act as if it were. Other countries, large and small, are partitioned for more or less the same reasons—India and Cyprus for example. In both these countries it has been shown that partition is still absolutely necessary, though it is worth noting that whereas Ulster showed that Britain had learned nothing from Cyprus, the Cyprus crisis of 1974 showed that both Turkey and Greece had learned a good deal from Ulster. Partition in these circumstances (we are not here concerned with the dismemberment of small nations by great powers where no internal division exists) is like a tourniquet applied to stop bleeding at a particular time and in specific circumstances. No one imagines it to be a permanent solution. It rarely satisfies either side, let alone both, and it has a great many practical disadvantages, especially economic ones. It might be said to have only one positive advantage, but that one is paramount. Partition is preferable to civil war.

The artificial division of so small an island as Ireland by the authority then responsible, the British government, inevitably suggests that the problem which dictated it is itself an artificial one, deliberately created by imperial interests outside Ireland, for political advantage of the most expedient and transient kind. No more misleading assumption could be made, and the consequence of such errors has been (and no doubt will be) the dangerous underestimation of the problem by successive generations of politicians, both Irish and British.

If we look only at the surface, the arguments against the creation of a separate administration for Northern Ireland would seem to be very strong; it does not appear to have a geographical or an ethnic *raison d'être*. In the first place it was brought into being simply by an Act of the Westminster Parliament which says that 'Northern Ireland shall consist of the parliamentary counties of Antrim, Armagh, Down, Fermanagh, Londonderry and Tyrone and the parliamentary boroughs of Belfast and Londonderry'.[1] This is in fact the only part of the Act which ever came into force, for the bill was originally framed to set up two governments in Ireland, one for the north and one for the south. Both were to remain within the United Kingdom, and a Council of Ireland was projected, whose efforts, it was hoped, would in time unite them. Northern Ireland was thus the by-product of a desperate attempt to solve the Irish question by compromise, and few states can have had a less satisfactory constitution.

Secondly, the state does not even consist of the whole province of Ulster, for three counties (Donegal, Monaghan and Cavan) are not included in it. A rather clumsy new name had to be found for it, Northern Ireland, which is both inaccurate (because of Donegal) and a rich source of confusion in Britain. Most people simply call it Ulster, but even this is regarded by Catholics as unionist propaganda. Moreover, most observers vaguely assume that the state coincides with the Plantation of Ulster of James I's reign. In fact the greatest concentration of Protestant population is in the eastern counties of Antrim and Down, which were not included in the six escheated counties of the plantation.

Again, home rule for Northern Ireland was a solution which no one wanted in 1920. At that stage, the Ulster unionists sought it as little as the nationalists or the British government. What the

Ulster Protestants wanted was to remain forever within the United Kingdom. It was really an ironic twist of events that gave them the home rule they had so resolutely opposed for Ireland as a whole. Ultimately, however, home rule came to seem to them to be the life raft on which they escaped when the unionist cause foundered.

Finally, all the inconsistencies might be explained if the population of Northern Ireland were homogeneous, if it consisted entirely of Protestants loyal to Britain. But a third of the population of Northern Ireland is Catholic, and, almost without exception, sympathetic to the ideal of a united and independent Ireland. In this respect the Ulster unionists have the worst of both worlds: the ratio of two to one in population is undoubtedly the most difficult, for it means that while the Protestants have always been absolutely sure of a safe majority in political matters, the Catholics know perfectly well that they are numerically strong enough to disrupt the state at any time if the price is worth paying. In the Irish Republic, on the other hand, the Protestant minority is so small in relation to the total population that the government has nothing to fear from it. Moreover, Protestants there accept the state and are loyal to it: they do not challenge the predominantly Catholic power structure. It ought to be said that, since independence, Protestants in the twenty-six counties have in the main been treated generously and well. It is very much in the interest of the Catholic majority that this should be so, and it is not difficult for the Irish government to ensure it, except in circumstances where intense popular feeling is aroused.

If one were to go no deeper, the case against partition would appear to be unanswerable, and it is scarcely surprising that it is so presented throughout the world. But the truth is that partition is not a line drawn on the map; it exists in the hearts and minds of Irish people,[2] a fact that was strikingly illustrated in the early stages of the Ulster troubles when soldiers had to draw a part of the border through the centre of Belfast. The border as a frontier between the United Kingdom and the Republic of Ireland is a very rough and ready attempt to follow the real division of the population, rougher indeed than it was ever intended to be (see p. 171 below). Nationalists may or may not be justified in their attempts to remove it and to annex the other six counties of Ireland to the Republic, but there is little point in so doing unless they can find a way to eliminate that other border in the mind.

Partition exists not because the entire population of one part of the country is in total disagreement with the population in the rest of it, but because a minority has been successful in asserting its right of dissent from the majority in the form of a separate administration and a constitutional boundary. This brings us at once to the question of minorities and what they can or cannot do. Discussion of the topic, however, is more often conducted in terms of what the minority *may* or *may not* do. In other words it is usually argued that minorities, though they have a right to toleration and equal citizenship, decidedly do not have a right to thwart the will of the majority and that this is especially true in the determination of the authority and boundaries of the state. Minorities are not permitted to set up their own states within the state as a whole. This is a perfectly fair and logical argument, and it is in accord with democratic principles as they are normally understood: religious and ethnic minorities in most countries are obliged to accept the will of the majority in return for toleration. The matter, however, is not as simple as this.

For one thing, if majority and minority are not agreed on basic principles no moral or legal criteria are applicable. The question then becomes one of what the minority can do *in the circumstances*, and it is settled in terms of political expediency. In any case, the minority has a good legal argument, since it can claim that it continues to recognise the lawfully constituted and unrevoked authority of a supreme, even if supranational, government. Whereas the majority has rebelled against that authority, gone outside its law, and achieved power by force of some kind, the loyalist minority can justly claim to have behaved correctly throughout, and never to have abandoned its allegiance. By no stretch of the imagination can it be deemed a crime to remain loyal to the civil government whose authority operated when one was born.

In nationalist eyes, however, loyalty to the British government is simply treason, and extremists, at least, have no doubts or qualms about the righteousness of this attitude. Nor is this position peculiar to Irish nationalists; it has been assumed by every nationalist movement which has asserted its claim against an imperial or colonial government. It acts on the dictates of an older, prescriptive, definition of nationhood deemed to have existed before the imperial subjugation took place. Thus it is perfectly possible for a loyalist population, particularly if it is a settler or colonist population, to find itself regarded as being in the 'immoral' position of thwarting the national will and taking sides with the wicked colonial oppressor. The French European population of Algeria, even though they were (like their parents and grandparents) in every sense as Algerian as African Algerians, and even though Algeria was legally not a colony but a part of metropolitan France, were in the end made foreigners and even traitors in the land of their birth. Rejected not only by Algerian nationalists but by France as well, they were forced by the struggle for national liberation to make the stark choice of either accepting the legality of the revolution or becoming despised refugees in their own motherland. That is the situation into which the I.R.A. hopes to manoeuvre the loyalists of Ulster. They are hopeful of eventual success. The world is on their side; even the imperialist enemy is on their side. They believe, or have been told, that 'the tide of history' is on their side. The example of Algeria, among many others, gives them every encouragement.

The tide of history, however, is not on anybody's side but its own, and it is subject to disconcerting eddies. Such a one has occurred in Ireland since about 1886. The historian cannot talk about the rightness of a national cause or the wrongness of a minority's resistance; such judgments are in any case more often than not the product of political cant, the hypocrisy which uses words to deceive, in order to achieve a political end. Other criteria must be applied. It must be remembered, for example, that Ireland is not Algeria, and that Northern Ireland is not Cyprus. The white Algerians were not at all in the same situation as the Protestants of Ulster, nor was their history the same. They were settlers in a sense that the Ulstermen are not. The difference between Christian and Muslim, between white-skinned and dark-skinned, is not that which exists between Catholic and Protestant in Ulster. Similar problems occur in many countries, but no two problems have all the same features. The Ulster problem is, when all is said and done, only the Ulster problem.

In the long run the one decisive factor in partition is not the weakness of Irish nationalism, nor the guile of unionists, nor the chicanery of British statesmanship. It is the simple determination of Protestants in north-east Ireland not to become a minority in a Catholic Ireland. It is towards weakening this determination that all the efforts of Irish nationalism ought in theory to have been aimed. Instead they have been largely directed to strengthening it in every possible way. The success of the Protestant minority has produced a bizarre consequence, for it has created within its own state a Catholic minority. The Ulster problem, as has been pointed out,[3] but not sufficiently comprehended, is in essence the problem of a *double* minority. Since 1969 a great deal has been said about 'the minority', but it is always the Catholic minority in the north which is meant. It seems hardly to occur to most observers that half the insecurity of the majority position stems from the basic anxieties which haunt a potential minority.

The course of Irish history, or of Anglo-Irish history, since the seventeenth century, has produced *two* religious minorities, but their experience has not been the same. After 1690 the Anglican Protestant population, though numerically a minority, was in fact a privileged élite who by law enjoyed a monopoly of political power in Ireland. They thought of themselves as the Irish nation, the Protestant nation. This is the only proper historical significance of the term Protestant Ascendancy, and as we have seen, the dissenting Protestants of eastern Ulster were no part of it and were indeed very hostile to it, except in the circumstance that the siege situation was re-created by some action of the excluded Catholic majority. (This was an important exception, of course, and one which often operated.) In spite of being a colonial population, a garrison (to use a term loaded with emotive significance for the rest of the population), the Ascendancy considered themselves distinctly Irish, and within the space of a century they enunciated and pressed on the home government a completely articulated Irish nationalism, which was actually to a large extent subsumed in the later Catholic nationalism of the nineteenth and twentieth centuries.

But in the nature of things it was a blind alley. It could not be further developed without Catholic emancipation and the widening of the franchise, and both of these reforms would inevitably have the effect of ending the Protestant nation. In the first half of the nineteenth century the Protestants, aware that they were becoming a minority in the political sense, ceased to be nationalists and clung to the union with Britain. In the long run they created unionism very largely in reaction to the new forms which Catholic nationalism was taking. In Ulster, however, this basic pattern was complicated, as we have already seen, by a number of cross-currents. If the Presbyterians ceased to be nationalists, they did not cease to be liberals, and they instinctively chose the opposite side politically from the Tories of the Established Church. Although conservative Presbyterians and Anglicans grew closer together, especially after Catholic emancipation, Liberalism (with a capital L) was still very strong in Ulster until 1886.

The Ulster question in its modern form appears to begin in that year when Gladstone introduced his first Home Rule Bill for Ireland in the House of Commons. Catholics in Ulster regarded the bill with the same high hopes as most of their co-religionists in the other three provinces, but the reaction of Ulster Protestants was immediately unfavourable. Whereas, in the rest of Ireland, opposition to the bill derived its support mainly from the middle and upper classes, in Ulster it had support from Protestants at every level of society. Anglicans and dissenters, landlords and tenants, industrialists and workers united in the common cause. They would not have home rule. This fact was of the utmost importance for the future. Until that time, well-to-do Protestants in Ulster had felt secure, but the general election revealed starkly the effect of the Franchise Act of 1884. Of the thirty-three Ulster Members of Parliament elected, seventeen were for, and sixteen against, home rule.

The subsequent course of Irish history was clearly indicated in the results of the 1886 election. What they indicated was partition, the exclusion of at least eastern Ulster from an independent, nationalist Ireland. The electoral map has hardly changed since, despite the myriad hopes wasted upon it. From 1886 until 1920 Ulster Protestants were again a minority under threat, and the history of Ireland in that period is shaped by their absolute determination not to become a minority in an independent, or even semi-independent, Catholic state.

*          *          *

'The six northern counties of Ireland are so very differently circumstanced from the rest, that they very well deserve a separate consideration, if there be really any intentions of restoring the tranquillity of the country.' This sentence was not written in the twentieth century. It appears in a pamphlet published shortly after the 1798 rebellion, and it serves as a salutary reminder that the idea of partition was not new in 1920. The author, an 'Irish country gentleman', goes on to say that the six counties are different from the rest because they are predominantly Presbyterian, and he adds that in England it is not understood how formidable the Presbyterians are in Ireland, and how active a part they took in the insurrection. In England 'all the disturbances in Ireland are referred to the Catholics only, but with very little truth; for had the Presbyterians been allowed to take the lead, it would not only have been called a Presbyterian instead of a Catholic rebellion, but I am afraid would have proved a Presbyterian revolution'. Events turned out differently, however, and 'the moment the Catholics acquired force, the Presbyterians took the alarm; the old jealousy and hatred of the Puritans to the Catholics revived in all its force in the breasts of their descendants'.[4] It must be remembered that this was written at a time when many of the Presbyterians, far from being loyalists, were in the van of the movement for Irish independence. By a curious coincidence, the word partition occurs in Drennan's best-known poem, 'When Erin first rose':

> Let my sons unite, like the leaves of the shamrock
> A partition of sects, from one footstalk of right.[5]

In Drennan, as in many of the Presbyterian radicals, pride in being an Ulster Protestant dissenter is mingled with Irish patriotism, and sometimes the two loyalties conflicted. Though he remained ardently anti-Orange and pro-Catholic for the whole of his life, Drennan often displayed a lack of trust in his Catholic allies (see pp. 108–9). His son, John Swanwick Drennan, who greatly admired his father, became a Liberal Unionist and wrote verses to celebrate unionist resistance to home rule in 1892.[6] The political independence of Ulster Presbyterians was always more significant than either their nationalism or their unionism, and this is still true today.

Partition was discussed from time to time during the nineteenth century, and the contrasts between Ulster and the rest of Ireland, which gave rise to it, were so apparent that travellers sometimes wrote as if it already existed. The German J. G. Kohl remarked in 1843 that coming into Ulster from the south was like crossing a frontier. 'The coach rattled over the boundary line, and all at once we seemed to have entered a new world. I am not in the slightest exaggerating, when I say that everything was as suddenly changed as if struck by a magician's wand.' Almost a century earlier, John Wesley had made much the same observation. 'No sooner did we enter Ulster than we observed the difference. The ground was cultivated as in England, and the cottages not only neat, but with doors, chimneys and windows.'[7]

Partition, as a practical way of dealing with the Irish question, was suggested by Macaulay in the House of Commons in 1833 in answer to O'Connell's demands for a repeal of the Union. He said: 'I defy the honourable and learned member to find a reason for having a parliament at Dublin which will not be just as good for having another Parliament at Londonderry.' The clearest ground he could guess at as the basis of O'Connell's repeal scheme would apply *a fortiori* to a separation of the legislatures of the north and south of Ireland, and the reasoning that only a domestic legislature could remedy a domestic grievance would apply tenfold in favour of a Parliament in Derry, 'or some other large town in the north of Ireland'.[8] The question was revived during the home rule controversy in 1886, when the demand for a separate legislature in the north was voiced by members of Gladstone's own party. In a speech at Birmingham on 21 April 1886 Joseph Chamberlain declared that because of the distinctions between north and south in 'race, religion and politics', he would be glad if 'there could be conceded to Ulster a separate assembly'.[9]

Gladstone's blindness to the strength of Protestant feeling in 1886 is hard to explain. He was of course anxious to minimize the difficulties in the way of his scheme, but it seems hardly credible that so astute a politician could have imagined that the Ulster problem would easily be set aside. In 1886, and again in 1893, Ulster Liberals, to whom Gladstone had been an idol, were infuriated by his offhand attitude to their arguments. His treatment of a deputation of Belfast businessmen in 1893, for example, was far from courteous. 'Jumping with impatience, he interrupted frequently and then launched into speech that lasted for almost three-quarters of an hour. His remarks were considered for the most part vague, generalized and historical, having little bearing on the points raised by the deputation, and gently insinuating "that our zeal to magnify the importance of our city had led us into egregious error".' The deputation concluded that Gladstone was mad, and found it 'positively shocking to see the hideous mechanical grin with which he took leave of us'.[10]

When Gladstone announced his proposals for home rule, Irish Protestants closed their ranks. Old divisions were forgotten; Presbyterian Liberals became Conservatives overnight, and the Orange Order was re-invigorated and made respectable by the return of aristocratic, clerical and middle-class support. At the time Protestants could see in home rule only their elimination from the Irish political scene. They believed that the Union would be replaced not only by the rule of a Dublin parliament but by the rule of the Catholic Church. They saw the Union as the only guarantee of their imperilled position and property, and clung to it the more fervently.

Two aspects in particular of this reaction have been misunderstood. One is the support given to the Ulster Protestant resistance by Lord Randolph Churchill and other Conservatives, who quickly saw party political advantage in the Irish situation. This intervention, later to be repeated by Bonar Law in even more dramatic circumstances, is sometimes represented by Irish historians as the cause of the division in the Irish nation. It was nothing of the sort.[11] Even if Conservative politicians had never taken up the Ulster cause, the Protestants would have behaved in the same way, and they were later to show that they were prepared to face any consequences with or without allies.

The second aspect is one which naturally follows, and which reinforces this view. It is sometimes assumed that the Protestant plans to resist by force of arms appeared first in the crisis of 1912–1914, but when we look more closely we find that this is not true. As far back as the 1860s the message had been that 'the black north can look after itself'; at the time of the Fenian crisis Ulster landlords were preparing to arm 'sound' tenants with 'very superior rifle arms'.[12] But it was in 1886 that the first co-ordinated proposals were made by Ulster Unionists, led by Colonel Saunderson, for resisting home rule by force. The Orange Order provided a convenient framework, not only for political organization, but if need be for a private army. Advertisements appeared in Belfast newspapers asking for rifles and drill instructors.[13]

The intensity of feeling against the bill was considerable, and in Belfast it took a markedly sectarian turn. The riots which broke out in the summer of 1886 were the worst the city had experienced, and many people were killed and injured. Saunderson's idea of organizing opposition on military lines was, like Carson's later, as much to impose discipline and order on such mobs as to make his determination clear to the government. The actual extent of Protestant military preparation at the time has been much underestimated.

## 2. Protestants, 1886–1925

In 1886, however, the issue was decided in the Commons. When in 1893 Gladstone introduced a second home rule bill, it passed through the Commons but was thrown out by the House of Lords. Once again there was great political excitement in Ulster, and further steps were taken towards a policy of active resistance. The solidarity of Protestant opinion had been expressed by a vast unionist convention in Belfast, accommodated in a building specially constructed for the occasion in the short space of three weeks. At this assembly the Duke of Abercorn asked his audience to repeat after him, 'We will not have home rule'; and Thomas Sinclair, formerly a Gladstonian Liberal, received enthusiastic cheers when he succinctly outlined a policy of passive resistance: 'We are children of the revolution of 1688, and, cost what it may, we will have nothing to do with a Dublin parliament. If it be ever set up we shall simply ignore its existence. Its acts will be but as waste paper; the police will find our barracks preoccupied with our own constabulary; its judges will sit in empty court-houses. The early effort of its executive will be spent in devising means to deal with a passive resistance to its taxation co-extensive with loyalist Ulster.'

Two years later the Conservatives were back in power in England and the agitation receded. The Ulster unionists remained on the alert, however, and in 1904 when Lord Dunraven (a southern unionist) produced a scheme for giving Ireland greater powers of self-government through partially elected councils, they reacted vigorously by setting up the Ulster Unionist Council which was for the future to direct the anti-home rule campaign in Ulster. The third home rule bill was introduced by Asquith in April 1912. By then the situation had altered in one vital respect. The Parliament Act of 1911 had reduced the veto of the House of Lords to three successive sessions, and the home rule bill was therefore certain to become law. It remained to be seen whether the unionists would resist it by other than constitutional methods. The answer was not long in coming.

In 1912 half a million Protestants signed an Ulster Covenant pledging themselves to resist home rule by any means. In 1913 an Ulster Volunteer Force was formed from units which had been drilling and arming since 1911, and arms were secretly imported to equip it. This citizen army, commanded by landowners and businessmen, and later by retired British Army officers, was extremely well organized and was prepared to take over the policing and defence of the whole Province of Ulster. Its numbers eventually reached almost 100,000, and it possessed cavalry, a motor-car corps, a special strike force, signallers and dispatch riders, and ambulance and nursing units. It lacked only artillery and aircraft. The unionists had their own communications system, and were in a position to seize the harbours, roads and railways of Ulster. They set up a Provisional Ulster Government to take control of the province on the day that the home rule bill passed. The 'Curragh Incident' of March 1914 further strengthened their position and weakened Asquith's, and in a dramatic coup in April they landed 26,000 rifles and 3,000,000 rounds of ammunition from Germany at Larne and other ports in eastern Ulster. All attempts made at negotiation and compromise failed and only the outbreak of the First World War averted a civil war in Ireland and possibly in Britain also.

In the early stages of this crisis, the total earnestness of the Ulster Protestants was not at first credited by the Liberal government or its supporters. The Protestants' assertion that home rule would threaten their religious freedom was dismissed as mere bigotry, and their resolve not to submit to it as bluff. In the end, it was believed, they would accept a *fait accompli*. English opinion derided the Orangemen with their wooden rifles and solemn religious fervour; but as the volunteers armed, and as their supporters in Britain turned increasingly to contemplate desperate measures to overthrow a government which would not go to the country for a mandate on the question, Englishmen realized too late that they had gravely underestimated the nature of the Ulster revolt. When a section of the army refused, in effect, to take action against the Ulster Volunteers, it was seen at last that the constitution had been shaken to its foundations.

In the course of the prolonged political crisis there occurred the gradual dissociation of the Ulster Protestants from unionists in the rest of Ireland, and the reluctant acceptance of the idea of partition. In 1913 Bonar Law wrote to Carson: 'I have long felt that if it were possible to leave Ulster as she is, and have some form of Home Rule for the rest of Ireland that is, on the whole, the only way out.' Carson replied: 'A difficulty arises as to defining Ulster. My own view is that the whole of Ulster should be excluded but the minimum would be the six plantation counties, and for that a good case could be made.'[14] (He meant the present six counties, not those of the plantation.)

The Ulster defiance of Westminster evoked a new militancy in Irish nationalism. Padraig Pearse said that the Orangeman with a rifle was a less ridiculous figure than the nationalist without one, and the journal of the Irish Republican Brotherhood declared that Carson was the only Irish M.P. with any backbone. The 1916 insurrection marked the turning point: thereafter Sinn Fein spoke increasingly for nationalist opinion, and in 1918 they annihilated the Nationalist Party at the polls. In the meantime there had been several unsuccessful attempts to solve the Irish difficulty on the basis of some kind of exclusion for all or part of Ulster, for a time or permanently. Ever since 1913 Lloyd George had been producing ingenious schemes to this effect, and when he became prime minister in 1916 he once again tried to bring nationalists and unionists to negotiate on the Ulster question, but this attempt failed, and so too did the promising Irish Convention of 1917, which, in addition, further divided the Ulster unionists from the southern unionists.

From 1917 on, however, it was clear that Lloyd George was unwilling to coerce the Ulster Protestants into accepting an all-Ireland parliament. 'To place them under national rule against their will', he said, 'would be as glaring an outrage on the principles of liberty and self-government as the denial of self-government would be for the rest of Ireland.'[15] This was the origin of the scheme embodied in the Government of Ireland Act of 1920. Lloyd George considered that there were four ways in which the Ulster demands could be met: by the exclusion of all Ulster; by county option, leaving substantial minorities outside the area excluded; by the exclusion of the six counties *en bloc*; or by such exclusion with provision for subsequent alteration of boundaries. When he made these proposals a savage guerrilla campaign was raging in Ireland, and he took the realistic view that the isolation of the Ulster problem was the first step towards solving the greater problem.

The 1920 act was rejected by Sinn Fein: since 1919 the Irish M.P.s (except those representing Dublin University) had constituted themselves as Dail Eireann. The Ulster unionists accepted the Act only as 'the supreme sacrifice' (to quote Sir James Craig).[16] Unionists outside the six counties were left to their fate, and the first Parliament of Northern Ireland was opened by King George V in 1921. In December of that year 'articles of agreement' were signed between the British government and the Sinn Fein leaders. Northern Ireland was allowed to opt out of the settlement and retain the status already enjoyed, but only on condition that, if she did, a Boundary Commission should be set up to determine the frontier between Northern Ireland and the Irish Free State.

When the Irish signatories to the treaty in 1921 agreed to the setting up of a Boundary Commission, they did so in the belief, which was not discouraged by Lloyd George, that it would recommend handing over to the south areas of such large extent that the northern state must collapse. Because of the troubles and the civil war the commission was not able to begin its work until the end of 1924. By that time neither the Free State nor Ulster was prepared to cede an inch of territory to the other.

Clause XII of the treaty had stipulated that the boundary was to

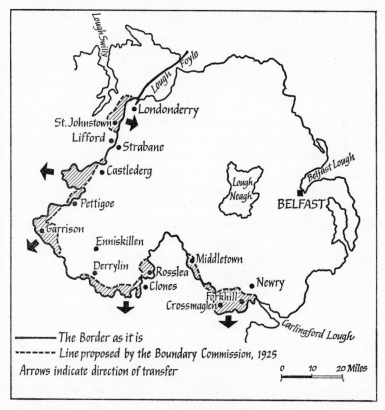

6 Changes to the border proposed by the Boundary Commission in 1925

be determined 'in accordance with the wishes of the inhabitants, so far as may be compatible with economic and geographical conditions'.[17] The neutral chairman of the commission, the South African judge Richard Feetham, interpreted this clause to mean that only such changes should be recommended as were compatible with the continued existence of the state of Northern Ireland, which had now survived as a devolved administration for almost four years. Craig's government refused to appoint a representative to the commission, however, on the ground that it was not a party to the treaty agreement, and the British government appointed the unionist J. R. Fisher, a former newspaper editor, to represent Northern Ireland. The Irish Free State representative, Professor Eoin MacNeill, though he did not of course support Mr. Justice Feetham's interpretation, did not formally dissent from it at this stage. The commission continued its work in secret for a year, and by November 1925 its report was ready. Then, on 7 November, the Conservative *Morning Post* published what it claimed were the commission's findings and a map of the redrawn boundary. The final award was seen to be much less unfavourable to Northern Ireland than had been expected. South Armagh and small areas of Fermanagh and Tyrone were to be given to the Free State, but Northern Ireland was to gain some parts of eastern Donegal (see map on p. 171).

The premature disclosure of these findings provoked a constitutional crisis which was resolved only by the hasty agreement of the three prime ministers of the United Kingdom, Northern Ireland and the Irish Free State to leave the border as it was, running round the parliamentary boundaries of the six counties. This compromise, however unsatisfactory, was preferred to the renewal of civil war, and the commission's report remained a secret document until 1968. The accuracy of the *Morning Post's* prediction was then confirmed. The 1920 border, longer, less logical and more vulnerable than that proposed by the commission, was not subsequently altered, and during successive I.R.A. campaigns it provided a major security problem for the Northern Ireland government. The outright warfare in the border areas since 1969 has inevitably suggested the possibility of redrawing it, and Northern Ireland would doubtless now be glad to give up the area of south Armagh around Crossmaglen and perhaps the western parts of Derry.

# 3. Catholics, 1920–1969

In 1920 the nature of the Ulster Protestants' problem was dramatically changed. Until that point they had feared becoming a minority in a Catholic state, and they desired to remain part of the Protestant majority in a United Kingdom. Now they were called upon to act as a majority, having to govern and tolerate a dangerously large and troublesome minority in a devolved administration which most Irishmen thought had no right to exist, without being able to divest themselves of any of the fears which went with being a minority. The Rev. J. B. Armour, a Presbyterian nationalist and a notable thorn in the side of his co-religionists, succinctly defined their dilemma. 'For years they have been yelling against Home Rule, and now they have got a form of Home Rule which the Devil himself could not have devised.'[18]

Though they did not want home rule for Ulster, the unionists made the best of the situation, and contrary to popular Catholic belief, they did genuinely try to create a nonsectarian state in which all citizens would enjoy equal rights. Carson, who declined to become Ulster's first prime minister, advised his followers to treat the Catholics well. They had every incentive to do so, for the continued existence of Northern Ireland depended on the Catholics at least tacitly recognizing its authority. It was clearly in the unionists' own interest to be able to show the rest of Ireland, Britain and the world that, having preserved their own religious freedom, as they saw it, they had no wish to interfere with that of anyone else. Above all, they needed to keep the goodwill of Britain, for they knew that the British could not understand their problems and easily became impatient at any display of what they considered to be religious bigotry.

The effort was probably doomed to failure, since one man's freedom is another's captivity, and the passions engendered by Irish history were too strong to evaporate in any system of secular government. As it was, events soon decided the issue by creating circumstances in which the nonsectarian ideal could not possibly survive.

The chief reason for its demise was the turmoil of the new state's early years. In 1969 it was all too easy for people to believe that Northern Ireland had been created merely by the stroke of a pen, and even to assume that it could be done away with by the same means. In fact the state called into existence by the 1920 Act forged its essential identity in bitter suffering and adversity, for the I.R.A. launched in the north a campaign of murder and outrage with the object of making it impossible for the new government to function. This inevitably set in train the ancient sectarian war. Most of the victims of the terror were innocent people shot down in the streets as they went about their ordinary business. Grenades were thrown into crowded tramcars, into pubs, into churches and even into groups of children playing at street corners. The response to I.R.A. shootings by infuriated sections of the Protestant population was sometimes on a larger scale, particularly after specific incidents such as the murder of District-Inspector Swanzy on the steps of a church in Lisburn. Whole streets were burned down, and in Belfast some main roads became like sections of the Western Front, still vivid in the memory of many of the combatants. Catholics alleged throughout the world that these attacks amounted to 'pogroms', and found a ready audience, especially in the United States. The sectarian rioting, superimposed on the conflict already existing between the I.R.A. and the British army, brought Ulster to a state of anarchy. It was a situation which led to the raising of a Protestant special constabulary to assist the R.U.C., the 'B-Specials', and the passing of emergency legislation to give the government special powers for dealing with terrorists, including the power of internment without trial.

The restoration of public order in 1923 owed much to two external factors. First, Sir James Craig, the Northern Ireland Prime Minister, met the I.R.A. leader, Michael Collins, in London, and agreed with him that if the operations of the I.R.A. in the north were ended, his government would do everything within its power to protect the lives and property of Catholics in Northern Ireland. This promise Craig and his successors kept, without regard to the Catholics' attitude to the state. The second factor which halted the bloodshed in Ulster was the outbreak of civil war in the south of Ireland, which gave the northern administration a much-needed respite. This was used to re-establish the rule of law; gunmen, Protestant and Catholic alike, were disarmed and brought to trial; and the political leadership of the majority was regained and preserved. In the uneasy aftermath of the troubles, the R.U.C. had to remain an armed police force, the B-Specials were kept in existence, and the 'special powers', which were originally intended only as a temporary measure, were periodically re-enacted.

The erection of these emergency features into the permanent structure of government has been a major grievance of the minority. Given the ruthless determination of the republicans to overthrow the Northern Ireland Parliament at Stormont by violence, and the atmosphere of bitterness left by the troubles, it is difficult to see how events could have taken a different course. The I.R.A. campaign and the fierce sectarian clashes which were the birth pangs of the Northern Ireland state were neither forgotten nor forgiven. Even if they had not occurred, however, it is in the highest degree unlikely that the two communities would have settled down in harmony.

In the first place, the minority did not see itself as a minority at all; it did not want to be a minority in a Protestant state, but part of the majority in Ireland. It saw no reason why it should even recognize the existence of such a state, a totally artificial creation, Catholics argued, which was given legality for the express purpose of making a Protestant majority that would not otherwise exist. In this respect the position of the Ulster Catholic is a very difficult one. While he may feel himself to be an Ulsterman, and while he may even see considerable advantages in remaining within the United Kingdom, he cannot accept the idea of the Ulster state, because as an Irishman and a Catholic he is bound by natural sentiment to the country of Ireland and to the communion of his church: his loyalties are national and supranational.

From the outset, therefore, Catholics simply refused to recognize the state. They regarded their subjection to it as temporary, and pinned all their hopes on the Boundary Commission. The tripartite agreement of 1925 was a bitter disappointment, especially to Catholics in the border areas who had regarded the transfer of their areas as inevitable. They now felt that they had been let down by the Free State government and were trapped in a unionist state which would always regard them as second-class citizens. More and more of them turned from moderate forms of nationalism to the uncompromising absolute of republicanism, and this further hardened unionist attitudes. For the first few years Catholics refused all allegiance to the new state: teachers declined to accept their salaries from the Ulster Ministry of Education,[19] and nationalist representatives would not take their seats at Stormont. Eventually, however, Catholics had to accept the *ipso facto* existence of Northern Ireland. In 1925 two nationalist M.P.s took their seats in Stormont and by 1927 the remaining eight followed. Only the two republicans remained outside. Though the nationalists became a vociferous and ever-vigilant opposition to unionist government, they refused until 1965 to assume the role of official Opposition, since that would have implied recognition of the constitution and the Crown. From 1925 the voice of Catholic complaint was never silent, and when Stormont was abolished by the British government in 1972 Catholics were essentially conducting the same arguments as their predecessors in the 1920s.

Broadly, the Catholics' grievances fell into two main categories. They alleged discrimination against them in the public service, in education, in housing and in employment, and argued that unionists had preserved their political dominance by the gerrymandering of electoral boundaries, most notoriously in the city of Derry. They also complained of direct repression by the apparatus of the state, in particular by the use of the special powers against republicans. The gravamen of the Catholic indictment, however, was that Catholics were completely excluded from the government of Northern Ireland, which remained a one-party and one-religion government for over half a century. Strangely, though this was demonstrably well-founded, it received before 1969 relatively little emphasis compared with the less provable grievance of discrimination.

The minority had no incentive to reform the state, since they did not want it to exist, and the accumulation of complaints created a picture of unrelieved blackness, of a people grievously oppressed and denied any means of redress. Catholic hatred of Stormont, of Unionist politicians, of the Orange Order, of the B-Specials, of the British flag and national anthem was total, unalleviated by any effort at compromise or understanding of the Protestant viewpoint. (It must be remembered that compromise has only been discussed by both sides since Westminster's intervention in 1969, and only in wake of the disorders.)

The problem for historians of the future will be to discover why the civil rights demonstrations of 1968 unleashed a sectarian war of unparalleled dimensions, reopened the Irish question and led to a guerrilla war between a vastly reinvigorated I.R.A. and the British army. They will hardly be satisfied that the answer is to be found in a cant phrase of the conflict, 'fifty years of unionist misrule'. Even if the unionists had used every opportunity for abuse of political power available to them between 1920 and 1972, the total of Catholic grievance far exceeds the unionist administration's actual capability to oppress the minority. Certain obdurate facts cannot be swept aside, though it may be argued that much is concealed by them. For instance, Northern Ireland remained a parliamentary democracy, in which government was conducted on the same lines as in the rest of the United Kingdom. It was never a police state, because the police, like every other branch of the executive, was subject to the scrutiny of Parliament. There was no question which could not be aired in Parliament. The press was not censored. With one important exception, there were no official curbs on free speech or the free expression of political opinion. The exception was the ban placed on the publication and distribution of republican and I.R.A. literature. Not only did Stormont not enact discriminatory laws against Catholics; it was expressly forbidden to do so by the 1920 Government of Ireland Act.[20] Westminster guaranteed the rights of the minority, and if they were in any way infringed, then Westminster and not Stormont was culpable.

Moreover the period of unionist rule was, with the exception of some ugly riots in the early 1930s, almost free of sectarian violence. This aspect of unionist government, though an important one, is rarely the subject of comment. The relative tranquillity of Northern Ireland between 1923 and 1968 is probably explained by the fact that the unionist government had the confidence, and therefore the control, of the Protestant population. It is significant that the determined I.R.A. campaign of 1956–61 failed both to gain the general support of the Catholic population and to provoke Protestant reprisals. Yet by 1969 a totally different atmosphere existed.

None of this alters the fact that the government lacked the consent of one-third of the population, and that in the interstices of an apparently free society many minor injustices could, and did, flourish. The cultivation of inequality, in practical day-to-day matters if not in law, was aided by the circumstance that Protestants were allowed, and indeed obliged, to claim the monopoly of loyalty to the government, quite apart from their loyalty to Britain. Thus each community had a ground of justified criticism of the other.

The Irish, Catholic and Protestant alike, are not prone to understate a grievance. This is one of the marked differences between the Irish and the English: the more injury is done to an Englishman, the less he will say about it, but with an Irishman the reverse is true. Once again, it is a trait which has long been observed. Fynes Morrison speaks in the sixteenth century of the Irish *skill* at complaining of injustice.[21] In 1612 Sir John Davies noted that 'all the common people have a whyning tune of Accent in their speech, as if they did still smart or suffer some oppression'.[22]

The point is that whatever specific complaints Catholics may have had about civil rights in Northern Ireland, the strength and peculiar bitterness (and even strange as it may seem, the very substance) of their grievance were derived from an experience quite outside the fifty years of unionist rule. This is equally true, as we have already seen, of Protestant political attitudes to the Catholic claims. To Catholics Stormont was a symbol. It took the place of Dublin Castle, and anyone who tried to co-operate with it automatically became a 'Castle Catholic'. They identified its legislation with the Penal Laws, and the unionist majority with the 'Protestant Ascendancy' of the eighteenth century. With Catholic politicians it is a commonplace to refer to the overthrow of the

'Protestant Ascendancy' in 1969. They are not necessarily trying deliberately to confuse the legal Ascendancy of the penal era with the democratic Protestant majority of Northern Ireland today, for even before the border was established it was noticed that in the north 'the shadow of the ascendancy of a bygone age seems to hang over the Catholics'.[23]

What the Catholics have been saying for fifty years about the Ulster government springs from a well that was made bitter long before Stormont was built. Again and again, if one reads carefully through the dreary and protracted debate, in the local press, or in the columns of the Stormont Hansard, one catches the echo of things Catholics said, and said repeatedly, before 1920: about the plantation, about the confiscation of land, about the Penal Laws, about Ribbonmen and Peep o'Day Boys, Hibernians and Orangemen, about outrage and riot, about flags and emblems, civil rights and second-class citizenship. The great strength of Catholic criticism of government is its ability to carry over into the local situation of today the inherited Catholic consciousness of the entire Anglo-Irish struggle since it began.

## 4. 'The Integrity of Their Quarrel'

After the end of the First World War, Winston Churchill expressed his impatience with the details of the religious geography which had played a large part in frustrating a settlement of the Ulster question in 1914. 'The whole map of Europe has been changed,' he wrote. 'The mode and thought of men, the whole outlook on affairs, the grouping of parties, all have encountered violent and tremendous changes in the deluge of the world, but as the deluge subsides and the waters fall we see the dreary steeples of Fermanagh and Tyrone emerging once again. The integrity of their quarrel is one of the few institutions that have been left unaltered in the cataclysm which has swept the world.'[24] At this point, whether he knew it or not, Churchill came close to defining the essential character of the Ulster problem.

Most people, if asked to define the chief symptoms of the Northern Ireland troubles, would say it is that the two communities cannot live together. The very essence of the Ulster question, however, is that they *do* live together, and have done for centuries. They share the same homeland, and, like it or not, the two diametrically opposed political wills must coexist on the same narrow ground. When all is said and done, Cain and Abel were brothers. There are certain strings which when touched evoke the same emotions in both peoples. Thus the reaction of both communities to the 'Londonderry Air' may be like that of the Swiss to the *ranz des vaches*, which, Hazlitt tells us, 'when its well-known sound is heard, does not merely recall to them the idea of their country, but has associated with it a thousand nameless ideas, numberless touches of private affection, of early hope, romantic adventure, and national pride, all which rush in (with mingled currents) to swell the tide of fond remembrance, and make them languish or die for home'.[25]

The unavoidable fact of coexistence dictates the most important aspect of the enduring conflict, which is that it must always be conducted in terms of topography. The exact cause of the quarrel, or more accurately of its survival, is often obscure to the onlooker. In many countries it is assumed that it is a holy war, *al jihad, Konfessionskrieg*,[26] and as such an abnormality in modernized societies, a sickening survival of a mediaeval religious rancour. The fact is, however, that the quarrel is not about theology as such and remains, in its modern form, stubbornly a constitutional problem, though religion is the shibboleth of the contending parties. Essentially the conflict in Ulster is not different from other conflicts in the modern world: it is about political power and who should wield it. People simply assume the political attitudes of the faith into which they were born. They rarely choose their political outlook after mature deliberation, and yet the entire debate on the question is conducted on the assumption that they do. Each side wastes its breath in trying to persuade the other to adopt its view of the situation, as if all men were reasonable creatures, and none the product of his environment and education.

Each community identifies itself with the myth it takes from Irish history. Each believes, mistakenly, that it still consists entirely of descendants of the Gaels or of the planters. In fact many of the

I.R.A. have planter surnames, and are probably of planter descent, while an Orangeman may be descended from Gaelic kings. Many who would defend Ulster's 'Protestant heritage' are sons or grandsons of Scots and English businessmen who settled in the province since 1900, while a foreign Catholic who settles in Ulster immediately identifies himself with Irish nationalism.

The segregation of the two religious communities, with the relative rarity of intermarriage, has preserved to a considerable extent the original mosaic of plantation, and population densities, except in Belfast, have remained surprisingly stable since the seventeenth century. The two communities are not intermingled— that is patently what has not happened—but they are interlocked, and in ways which it is probably impossible for anyone except the native of Ulster to understand. This gives rise to a situation in which the 'territorial imperative' is extremely insistent. The quarrel is therefore very much concerned with the relationship of people to land, and that relationship has indeed been considered the central theme of Irish history.[27]

Of its very nature it consists in particulars, the location of a road, a stretch of wall, a church or a cluster of houses, and the pattern has less relevance to abstract concepts of reconciliation, political reform, constitutional innovations, and this or that form of doctrinaire nationalism or unionism than is commonly supposed. Yet the problem is invariably discussed in abstract terms. The war in Ulster is being fought out on a narrower ground than even the most impatient observer might imagine, a ground every inch of which has its own associations and special meaning.

The Ulsterman carries the map of this religious geography in his mind almost from birth. He knows which villages, which roads and streets, are Catholic, or Protestant, or 'mixed'. It not only tells him where he can, or cannot, wave an Irish tricolour or wear his Orange sash, but imposes on him a complex behaviour pattern and a special way of looking at political problems. The nuance is all-important. If you cannot spell Donegall Place or Shankill Road correctly, if you do not know the vital difference between the Shankill district of Belfast and the Shankill district of Lurgan, you can scarcely hope to know what goes on in the minds of the people who live there.[28] To understand the full significance of any episode of sectarian conflict, you need to know the precise relationship of the locality in which it occurred to the rest of the mosaic of settlement. But the chequerboard on which the game is played has a third dimension. What happens in each square derives a part of its significance, and perhaps all of it, from what happened there at some time in the past. Locality and history are welded together. The perduring quality of local patterns of reaction almost defies a rational explanation, and is certainly underestimated to a remarkable degree. Why, for example, should Armagh, the most populous and prosperous of the Ulster counties, be notorious for ambush and outrage since the late eighteenth century, and why should judges in the nineteenth century find the Crossmaglen area especially notorious for murder and outrage? Why should Portadown and Lurgan have a history of sectarian rioting, like Belfast? And why should certain border villages, such as Rosslea or Garrison or Forkhill have been the scene of frequent confrontations and incidents long before there was any border?

# Prospect

The attempt which has been made to trace in Northern Ireland's recent conflict patterns of behaviour and attitude which are ingrained and of considerable antiquity might suggest a misleading conclusion. The reader who has come this far may assume that these patterns are held to be the actual cause of the crisis, but this is not so. Every nation, and every community, has similar patterns in the grain of its fabric, but not every one is undergoing the same turmoil. The most widespread, and most erroneous, assumption made about the Ulster crisis is that it is created entirely by Irish history, by the inability, that is, of Ulster people to free themselves from the problems of the past and address themselves to those of the present and of the future.

One might argue, however, that the conflict, at least in the beginning, was not the consequence of Irish history at all, nor of the basic instability of Northern Ireland's political institutions, but of tangible pressures and problems of the contemporary world. The outbreak of guerrilla warfare in Ulster was more closely linked with the *evenéments* of May 1968 in Paris, for example, than it was with the Penal Laws or the Battle of the Boyne. One of the many aspects of the political crisis was the contemporary fashion of mass protest in the streets which has led to such apparently disparate results as the Czechoslovak rising, the anti-Vietnam War campaign in the United States and the protracted political crisis in Portugal. Significantly, the act of triggering the seismic catastrophe in Northern Ireland was carried out by a generation too young to have any possible realization of the nature and consequences of previous Irish troubles.

The argument here is that once these contemporary pressures have operated, the form and course of the conflict are determined by patterns concealed in the past, rather than by those visible in the present. There is nothing unusual about such atavism as an aspect of human history. What is remarkable is that it should be so universally ignored. Not only are the lessons of the past disregarded; the community is actually instructed on all sides to disregard them, and at all costs. The ancestral voices in this case are false and wicked voices, and prophesy only war. Even if the community succeeded in forgetting the past, however, it is not likely that the past would forget it. The consequences of ignoring basic precepts are now all too obvious. 'The Gods of the Copybook Headings in fire and slaughter return.'[29]

The point may be illustrated by analogy. The average citizen of San Francisco is very little interested in the actual details of how people behaved during the earthquake which destroyed the city in 1906. That is now as much a subject for the specialist as the relevant seismology. Scientists tell us that because of the unstable character of the earth's crust along the San Andreas Fault an earthquake could occur again in San Francisco at any time. If such a disaster should take place, the details of how people actually behaved in 1906 might suddenly become of paramount importance for every citizen. In theory, all the scientific capability of the world's most technically advanced state would be applied to alleviate the consequences: the rescue services would be infinitely more effective than those of 1906. In practice, the efficiency of such systems would probably break down at a fairly early stage, and humanity, as always, would be thrown back on its inherent resources. In such circumstances the urban population would turn instinctively to the folk-memory of what was done before, and this might prove to be a factor of enormous importance in the evacuation of the city, the organizing of shelter, and the enforcement of obedience to instructions by the army and police. In desperate situations, when the normal framework of social order breaks down, ordinary people are rarely as lacking in common sense as those who govern them; the instinct for self-preservation is too strong.

Such a situation was created in Northern Ireland in 1969. Quite apart from the strong political passions involved, the population in both communities realized at an early stage of the troubles that the authorities were failing to contain the disturbances, and indeed that they did not understand their essential nature. The disarming of the police, and its temporary transformation from a law enforcement agency into a vulnerable and subordinate element of the

'security forces', was in itself a profound shock to society. For the
time being, the state had lost the capacity to safeguard life and
property, and, stripped of that protection, the civil population
turned instinctively to the only source of wisdom applicable to
such circumstances—the inherited folk-memory of what had been
done in the past, both good and bad. This atavism explains the
emergence of patterns of behaviour which seemed to have little
relevance to life in Northern Ireland between 1921 and 1969, but
which were very familiar to the historian.

What this amounts to is the delineation of patterns which cannot
be changed or broken by any of the means now being employed to
'solve' the Ulster question. Neither pressure from London, nor
pressure from Dublin, can alter them. They are impervious to
propaganda and to hostile criticism; since both must in the end
come to terms with the reality of their existence. Nor will they be
changed in essence by the economic, social and intellectual pressures of the contemporary world, as so many imagine. To say this
is not to aver that the economic and constitutional situation of
Northern Ireland will not change, or that its society will not change;
it is, of course, changing continually, but it changes in accord with
intrinsic laws, and not at the dictate of the makers of instant
blueprints. The function of wise constitutions and just reforms is
to help humanity to achieve a future that is better than the past, but
if they are not to have the opposite effect they must take account of
the grain, not cut against it. 'Prudent men are in the habit of
saying', wrote Machiavelli, 'that he who wishes to see what is to
come should observe what has already happened. . . . Future
things are also easily known from past ones if a nation has for a
long time kept the same habits.'[30] Or, as Ecclesiastes has it, 'All
the rivers run into the sea; yet the sea is not full; unto the place
from whence the rivers come, thither they return again.'[31]

# Notes and References

## Abbreviations

C.S.P.I.   Calendars of State Papers, Ireland.

H.M.C.   Historical Manuscripts Commission.

I.H.S.   Irish Historical Studies.

I.M.C.   Irish Manuscripts Commission.

In the Notes titles of works cited are given in abbreviated form. The full titles appear in the List of Sources.

# Notes

## Part One: Problems of Plantation

**1.** In March 1615 James told Chichester that he was 'discontented at the slow progress of that plantation, some few only of the seritors and natives having as yet performed the conditions of the plantation; the rest (for the greater part) having either done nothing at all, or so little, or by the reason of the slightness thereof to so little purpose, that the work seems rather to be forgotten by them, and to perish under their hand, than to be advanced; some having begun and not planted, others begun to plant and not build, and all of them in general retaining the Irish style, the avoiding of which was with him the fundamental reason of that plantation.' C.S.P.I. (1615–25), p. 25. For complaints against the Londonderry plantation on the same grounds by Sir Thomas Phillips, see *Londonderry and the London Companies, 1609–29*: 'The Londoners . . . who besides their workmen have brought over never a man to inhabit' (p. 34), and T. W. Moody, *Londonderry Plantation, passim*.

**2.** T. W. Moody, 'The treatment of the native population under the scheme for the plantation in Ulster', in I.H.S., vol. i, no. 1 (1938), pp. 59–63, and *Londonderry Plantation*, pp. 110–11, 331–5.

**3.** C.S.P.I. (1625–32), pp. 510–13. The Bishop of Derry complained that the Earl of Abercorn and his tenants were settling Scottish Catholics in and around Strabane. 'Sir George Hamilton has done his best to plant popery there, and has brought over priests and Jesuits from Scotland.'

**4.** Maxwell, *Sources*, p. 145.

**5.** *The Scotsman*, 2 Nov. 1911; quoted in McNeill, *Ulster's Stand for Union*, p. 101.

**6.** Evans, 'Irishness of the Irish', pp. 2–3.

**7.** Ibid., p. 5.

**8.** Ibid., p. 6.

**9.** *Archaeological Survey of Co. Down*, p. xiii.

**10.** For the 'Enterprise of Ulster' see Morton, *Elizabethan Ireland*, pp. 34–7, and *History Today*, vol. 17 (1967), pp. 114–21. Sir Thomas Smith's plan is in Dewar, *Sir Thomas Smith*, pp. 164–8.

**11.** Heslinga, *Irish Border*, p. 118.

**12.** Ibid., pp. 113–14. See also Moore, *Irish Sea Province*.

**13.** Heslinga, *Irish Border*, p. 137.

**14.** 'The Scotch are busily inhabiting a great part of Ulster, and must be driven away.' Henry VIII, *Letters and Papers*, vol. vi, p. 645; and see especially vols. xiii–xxi (1538–46), *passim*. Statutes, Ireland, vol. i, p. 274; Percival-Maxwell, *Scottish Migration*, p. 4.

**15.** Hill, *Montgomery Manuscripts*, p. 58.

**16.** The best succinct account of exactly where the Scots and English settled in the Ulster counties is by Professor J. Braidwood 'Ulster and Elizabethan English, I. Historical Introduction: the planters' in *Ulster Dialects*, pp. 5–45.

**17.** Davies, *Discoverie*, p. 3.

### Part Two: Signals of Siege

**1.** '*The soil of Ireland*', declared the proclamation of the Fenian provisional government in 1867, '. . . belongs to us, the Irish people, and to us it must be restored' (Lee, *Irish Society*, p. 54).

**2.** C.S.P.I. (1609), p. 196; Hill, *Plantation*, p. 350; Falls, *Birth of Ulster*, p. 211.

**3.** Sir Hugh Clotworthy to Lord Falkland, 16 February 1627, in C.S.P.I. (1625–32), p. 218.

**4.** The two plantations were frequently compared. See, for example, Percival-Maxwell, *Scottish Migration*, p. 138: 'Our plantations go on, the one doubtfully, the other desperately.' Chichester declared: 'I had rather labour with my hands in the plantation of Ulster than dance and play in that of Virginia' (Morton, *Elizabethan Ireland*, p. 101).

**5.** *Calendar of Carew MSS* (1603–23), p. 308.

**6.** See Froude's introduction to Hickson, *Ireland in the Seventeenth Century*, pp. i–xii.

**7.** Macaulay, *History*, vol. ii, p. 584.

**8.** Heslinga, *Irish Border*, p. 61.

**9.** Milligan, *Walls*, vol. 1, pp. 6–7.

**10.** So described in a letter from the lords of the council to Sir Arthur Chichester, 8 March 1608; in C.S.P.I. (1606–8), p. 435. '. . . They think it a kind of justice to that ominous place, to recommend him to look to the care thereof . . .'

**11.** Milligan, *Walls*, vol. i, p. 10.

**12.** C.S.P.I. (1647–60), p. 325.

**13.** Milligan, *Walls*, vol. i, p. 61.

**14.** *Report of Londonderry Riots Commission, 1869*, p. 60.

**15.** I.M.C., *Letters and Papers relating to the Irish Rebellion, 1641–6*, pp. 3–4.

**16.** Milligan, *Walls*, vol. i, p. 65.

**17.** Ibid, vol. ii, p. 33–6. 'If we put the thing in military terms, it is almost farcical: a larger, better-equipped force contained behind its walls by a smaller and worse-equipped one' (Belloc, *James II*, pp. 244–5). 'The plain fact is that there was no siege in the accepted meaning of the term, not even a blockade' (Petrie, 'Jacobite War', p. 43).

**18.** Milligan, *Siege*, pp. 21–2.

**19.** Witherow, *Derry and Enniskillen*, p. 29.

**20.** Hill, *Montgomery Manuscripts*, p. 273. During the siege the Presbyterians were allowed the use of the Cathedral for their services on Sunday afternoons. The publication of Walker's *Account*, and Mackenzie's reply, each claiming the decisive role in the defence for his co-religionists, 'set going an unpleasant post-siege controversy, which makes clear the ill-feeling between Scots and English colonists in seventeenth-century Ulster' (Simms, *Jacobite Ireland*, pp. 100–101).

21. J. A. Read, Introduction to Milligan, *Siege*, p. ix.
22. Michelburn, 'Ireland Preserv'd', quoted in Milligan, *Siege*, p. 372.
23. Witherow, *Derry and Enniskillen*, p. 34.
24. *Belfast Newsletter*, 10 April 1912.
25. Simms, *Jacobite Ireland*, p. 101.
26. Walker, *Account*, p. 31.
27. Ibid., p. 30.
28. Ibid., p. 32.
29. Macaulay, *History*, vol. ii, pp. 582–3.
30. Ibid., vol. ii, p. 585.
31. *Report of Londonderry Riots Commission, 1869*, p. 16.
32. Graham, *Siege*, pp. 286–7.
33. Inglis, *Tour*, vol. ii, p. 200.
34. J. L. McCracken, 'Early Victorian Belfast', in Beckett and Glasscock, pp. 96–7.
35. *Report of Londonderry Riots Commission, 1869*, p. 15.
36. *Report of Londonderry Riots Commission, 1883*, p. ix.

## Part Three: The Politics of Presbytery

1. Stewart, *History*, pp. 313, 315.
2. Reid, *History*, vol. i, pp. 97, 101.
3. Ibid., vol. ii, p. 116n.
4. Mansergh, *Irish Question*, p. 184.
5. Barkley, *Short History*, p. 8.
6. Witherow, *Memorials*, vol. i, p. 20.
7. Glover, *Scotland*, p. 162.
8. Adair, *True Narrative*, pp. 133–4; Beckett, *Modern Ireland*, p. 98.
9. Milton, *Prose Works*, vol. iii, pp. 297–9.
10. Ibid., vol. iii, p. 334.
11. Ibid., vol. iii, pp. 317, 322.
12. Adair, *True Narrative*, p. 252.
13. Reid, *History*, vol. iii, p. 405.
14. Ibid., vol. iii, pp. 431–2.
15. Ibid., vol. iii, p. 433.
16. This view is put forward in Rodgers, 'Carlile', pp. 52–3.
17. Reid, *History*, vol. iii, p. 111.
18. Ibid., vol. iii, p. 121.
19. *Rutland MSS*, vol. iii, p. 421.
20. Chart, *Drennan Letters*, p. 70.
21. Tone, *Autobiography*, vol. i, pp. 104–5, 113–14.

**Part Four: Patterns of Conflict**

1. Rev. J. Good, quoted in Introduction to Derricke, *Image*, p. ix.
2. Stevenson, *Two Centuries*, pp. 22–3.
3. Wesley, *Journals*, vol. iii, p. 486.
4. Scott, *Journal*, p. 3.
5. Kohl, *Ireland*, 129.
6. Derricke, *Image*, lines under Plate 2.
7. Maureen Wall, 'The Whiteboys', in Williams, *Secret Societies*, p. 192, n. 14.
8. Ibid., p. 16; Lewis, *Local Disturbances*, pp. 219–20.
9. Young, *Tour*, vol. i, p. 64.
10. Lecky, *History*, vol. iv, p. 12.
11. Sullivan, *New Ireland*, vol. i, pp. 226–7.
12. Lewis, *Local Disturbances*, p. 91; Donnelly, *Landlord and Tenant*, p. 30.
13. J. Lee, 'The Ribbonmen', in Williams, *Secret Societies*, p. 33.
14. Ibid., p. 32.
15. Trench, *Realities*, pp. 115–27.
16. Ibid., p. 116.
17. Ibid., p. 177.
18. Ibid., p. 119.
19. Steele, *Irish Land*, p. 19, and review in the journal *History*, (June 1972) p. 242.
20. The question is discussed in an interesting article by P. Gibbon, 'Orange Order'.
21. Crawford, *Domestic Industry*, p. 26.
22. Gibbon, 'Orange Order'.
23. MacDonagh, *Irish Life*, p. 53.
24. O'Donnell, *Irish Faction Fighters*, gives some very interesting details of these feuds. For the 'wheel' see pp. 19–20. W. R. Le Fanu (brother of the novelist Sheridan Le Fanu) declares that coat-trailing was a myth, arising from a misunderstanding of the 'wheel'. This would seem to be probable. See Le Fanu, *Seventy Years*, pp. 33–8.
25. *Reports from Select Committee on Orange Lodges, 1835, First Report*, p. 33. For the origins of Orangeism see also Senior, *Orangeism*, pp. 1–21, and McClelland, *Formation*, p. 2.
26. J. Byrne, 'An Impartial Account of the Late Disturbances in the County of Armagh' (1792), in Crawford and Trainor, *Aspects*, pp. 171–173.
27. *Charlemont MSS*, vol. ii, pp. 79–80.
28. Moore, *Truth About Ulster*, p. 11.
29. G. Steiner, in *The Listener*, 4 January 1973, p. 2.
30. Whyte, *Independent Irish Party*, p. 59. For the frequency of sectarian riots in Lancashire, 1850–70, see J. Vincent, *Origins of the Liberal Party*, p. 298.
31. *Illustrated London News*, 15 August 1872.
32. Moore, *Truth About Ulster*, pp. 20–21.
33. The only book entirely devoted to the history of Belfast riots is A. Boyd, *Holy War in Belfast*. Though vividly written, it exhibits strong

political prejudices, For a more balanced account see Budge and O'Leary, *Belfast*, pp. 72–100.

34. Moore, *Truth About Ulster*, p. 15. On at least one occasion Daniel O'Connell referred to Ireland as 'the volcanic land' (*Reports from Select Committee on Orange Lodges, 1835, Third Report*, p. 36).

35. Joy, *Historical Collections*, pp. 293–6; Boyd, *Holy War*, p. 3.

36. Boyd, *Holy War*, pp. 1–10.

37. For the segregation of the population of Belfast, see Jones, *Social Geography* and 'Belfast'.

38. Giraldus Cambrensis remarks that the Irish 'hurl stones against the enemy in battle with such quickness and dexterity that they do more execution than the slingers of any other nation' (*Topography of Ireland*, vol. iii, ch. 10, in Wright, *Historical Works of Giraldus Cambrensis*, p. 124).

39. Moore, *Truth About Ulster*, pp. 23–4.

40. Ibid., p. 25.

41. Ibid., p. 45.

42. Reminiscences of Robert Young transcribed by A. McClelland from MSS in the Linenhall Library (*Irish Booklore*, vol. 1, no. 1, January 1971).

43. Moore, *Truth About Ulster*, pp. 62–3. Among the soldiers stationed in Belfast in 1886 was the young Baden-Powell, who, as an officer in the Hussars, was billeted in a villa on the Falls Road. (*Belfast Telegraph*, 26 November 1974.)

44. Moore, *Truth About Ulster*, p. 69.

45. *Report of Belfast Riots Commission, 1857*, p. 5.

46. *Report of Belfast Riots Commission, 1864*, p. 19.

47. *Report of Belfast Riots Commission, 1857*, p. 8.

48. Boyd, *Holy War*, p. 206.

49. Buckland, *Ulster Unionism*, p. 37.

50. *Report of Belfast Riots Commission, 1886*, p. 16.

51. Budge and O'Leary, *Belfast*, p. 89.

## Part Five: Modes of Minority

1. Mansergh, *Irish Question*, p. 209.

2. 'The real partition of Ireland is not on the map but in the minds of men' (Beckett, *Short History*, p. 176).

3. Jackson, *Two Irelands, passim*.

4. Quoted in Heslinga, *Irish Border*, pp. 196–7.

5. W. Drennan, 'Erin'. *Belfast Monthly Magazine*, Oct. 1812, pp. 301–2.

6. J. S. Drennan, 'We meet: a voice from the Ulster convention, June 17th, 1892', in *Poems*, pp. 177–8.

7. Kohl, *Travels*, vol. i, p. 194; Wesley, *Journals*, 19 July 1756.

8. *Hansard*, 3rd series, vol. xv, col. 259.

9. Chamberlain, *Speeches*, vol. i, p. 271.

10. Buckland, *Ulster Unionism*, p. 14.

**11.** In reality, the Conservatives were not anxious to provoke a crisis in Ulster. See Cooke and Vincent, *Governing Passion*, p. 160.

**12.** Buckland, *Ulster Unionism*, pp. xxxv, 12.

**13.** *Northern Whig*, 18 June 1892.

**14.** Hyde, *Carson*, p. 342.

**15.** *Hansard*, 5th series, vol. cxxiii, col. 1171.

**16.** Sir James Craig to the Prime Minister, 11 November 1921 (Cmd. paper 1561).

**17.** Articles of agreement for a Treaty between Great Britain and Ireland (Cmd. paper 1560).

**18.** W. S. Armour, *Life of J. B. Armour*, p. 332, quoted in Lyons, *Ireland Since the Famine*, p. 682.

**19.** Akenson, *Education*, pp. 44–5.

**20.** Government of Ireland Act, 1920. Clause 4.

**21.** Falkiner, *Illustrations*, p. 308.

**22.** Davies, *Discoverie*, p. 176.

**23.** Moore, *Truth About Ulster*, p. 136.

**24.** Churchill, *Aftermath*, p. 319.

**25.** William Hazlitt, 'On genius and common sense', in *Table Talk*, p. 35n. The playing of the *ranz des vaches* in companies of Swiss mercenaries was forbidden on pain of death because of its effect on them. (*Belfast Monthly Magazine*, April 1810, p. 371.)

**26.** See, for instance, Vogt.*Konfessionskrieg*.

**27.** Beckett, *Irish History*, p. 15: 'We have, therefore, an element of stability—the land, and an element of instability—the people. It is to the stable element that we must look for continuity.'

**28.** Donegall with two l's, from the old spelling of the title of the Chichester family, Earls of Donegall. Shankill, being derived from the Irish for 'white church', has nothing to do with a hill, but is frequently mis-spelled. The Shankill area of Belfast is Protestant, that of Lurgan Catholic.

**29.** Kipling, 'The Gods of the Copybook Headings'.

**30.** *The Discourses*, chapter 43. Trans. A. H. Gilbert.

**31.** Ecclesiastes, I, 7.

# List of Sources

Adair, P.  *A True Narrative of the Rise and Progress of the Presbyterian Church in Ireland, 1623–70*. And Stewart, *History* (see below), ed. W. D. Killen, Belfast, 1866.

Akenson, D. H.  *Education and Enmity: The Control of Schooling in Northern Ireland, 1920–50*. Newton Abbot and New York, 1973.

*The Archaeological Survey of Co. Down*. Belfast, 1966.

Armour, W. S.  *Armour of Ballymoney*.  London, 1934.

Barkley, J.  *A Short History of the Presbyterian Church in Ireland*. Belfast, 1959.

Beckett, J. C.  *The Study of Irish History*. Inaugural lecture, Queen's University, Belfast. Belfast, 1963.

Beckett, J. C.  *The Making of Modern Ireland*. London, 1966.

Beckett, J. C., and Glasscock, R.  *Belfast: Origin and Growth of an Industrial City*. London, 1967.

*Belfast Monthly Magazine*, 1808–15.

*Belfast Newsletter*. 10 April 1912.

*Belfast Telegraph*. 26 November 1974.

Belloc, H.  *James II*. London, 1928.

Boyd, A.  *Holy War in Belfast*. Tralee, 1969.

Buckland, P.  *Ulster Unionism and the Origins of Northern Ireland, 1886–1922*. Dublin and New York, 1973.

Budge, I., and O'Leary, C.  *Belfast: Approach to Crisis. A Study of Belfast Politics, 1613–1970*. London, 1973.

Butler, W. F. T.  *Confiscation in Irish History*. Dublin, 1917.

*Calendar of the Carew Manuscripts Preserved in the Archiepiscopal Library at Lambeth, 1515–1624*. 6 vols. London, 1867–73.

*Calendars of State Papers, Ireland, 1509–1669*. London, 1860–1908.

Chamberlain, J.  *Speeches*, ed. C. W. Boyd. 2 vols. London, 1914.

*Charlemont MSS*. H.M.C., 12th Report, part x, and 14th Report, part viii. 2 vols. London, 1891–4.

Chart, D. A., ed.  *The Drennan Letters*. Belfast, 1931.

Churchill, W. S.  *The World Crisis. The Aftermath*. London, 1929.

Cmd. 1560 of 1921: Articles of Agreement for a Treaty Between Great Britain and Ireland.

Cmd. 1561 of 1921: Correspondence between His Majesty's Government and the Prime Minister of Northern Ireland relating to proposals for an Irish settlement.

Colles, R.  *The History of Ulster from the Earliest Times to the Present Day*. 4 vols. London, 1919–20.

Colvin, I.  *The Life of Lord Carson*. 3 vols (vol. 1 by E. Marchbanks). London, 1934.

Cooke, A. B., and Vincent, J.  *The Governing Passion*. London, 1974.

Crawford, W. H. *Domestic Industry in Ireland*. Dublin, 1972.

Crawford, W. H., and Trainor, B. *Aspects of Irish Social History, 1750–1800*. Belfast, 1969.

Davies, Sir John. *A Discoverie of the True Causes why Ireland was Never Entirely Subdued*. London, 1612 (reprint, Shannon, 1969).

Derricke, J. *The Image of Irelande with a Discouerie of Woodkarne, 1581*, ed. J. Small, with notes by Sir Walter Scott, Edinburgh, 1883.

Dewar, Mary. *Sir Thomas Smith*. Oxford, 1964.

Donnelly, J. S. *Landlord and Tenant in Nineteenth-Century Ireland*. Dublin, 1973.

Drennan, J. S. *Poems and Sonnets*. London, 1895.

Evans, E. E. 'The Irishness of the Irish'. Irish Association for Cultural, Economic and Social Relations, Belfast, 1967.

Evans, E. E. *The Personality of Ireland: Habitat, Heritage and History*. Cambridge, 1973.

Falkiner, C. L. *Illustrations of Irish History and Topography, Mainly of the Seventeenth Century*. London, 1904.

Falls, C. *The Birth of Ulster*. London, 1936.

Gibbon, P. 'The Origins of the Orange Order and the United Irishmen'. In *Economy and Society*, vol. 1 (1972).

Glover, Janet R. *The Story of Scotland*. London, 1960.

Graham, Rev. John. *A History of the Siege of Londonderry and Defence of Enniskillen in 1688 and 1689*. Dublin, 1829.

Hamilton, Lord Ernest. *The Irish Rebellion of 1641*. London, 1920.

*Hansard*. 3rd and 5th series.

Hazlitt, W. *Table Talk* (Everyman edition) London, 1969.

Heslinga, M. W. *The Irish Border as a Cultural Divide*. Assen, 1971.

Hickson, Mary. *Ireland in the Seventeenth Century, or the Irish Massacres of 1641–2*. London, 1884.

Hill, G. *An Historical Account of the Plantation in Ulster at the Commencement of the Seventeenth Century, 1608–20*. Belfast, 1877 (reprint Shannon, 1970).

Hill, G., ed. *The Montgomery Manuscripts, 1603–1706*. Belfast, 1869.

Hogan, J., ed. *Letters and Papers Relating to the Irish Rebellion, 1642–46*. (Irish Manuscript Commission) Dublin, 1936.

Hyde, H. M. *Carson*. London, 1953.

*Illustrated London News*. 15 August 1872.

Inglis, H. D. *A Tour Throughout Ireland in the Spring, Summer and Autumn of 1834*. 2 vols. London, 1835.

Jackson, H. *The Two Irelands: The Problem of the Double Minority*. Minority Rights Group. London, 1971.

Jones, E. 'Belfast. A Survey of the City'. In *Belfast in Its Regional Setting*. British Association. Belfast, 1952.

Jones, E. *A Social Geography of Belfast*. Oxford, 1960.

[Joy, H.] *Historical Collections Relative to the Town of Belfast*. Belfast, 1817.

Kohl, J. G. *Travels in Ireland*. London, 1843.

Lecky, W. E. H. *A History of Ireland in the Eighteenth Century*. 5 vols. London, 1892.

Lee, J. *The Modernization of Irish Society 1848–1918*. Dublin, 1973.

Le Fanu, W. R. *Seventy Years of Irish Society*. London, 1896.

*Letters and Papers of the Reign of Henry VIII*. London, 1862–1932.

Lewis, G. C. *On Local Disturbances in Ireland*. London, 1836.

Lyons, F. S. L. *Ireland Since the Famine*. London, 1971.

Macaulay, T. B. *A History of England from the Accession of James II*. 4 vols. London, 1848–61 (reprint, London, 1967).

McClelland, A. *The Formation of the Orange Order* (privately printed). Belfast, n.d.

MacDonagh, M. *Irish Life and Character*. London, 1899.

Mackenzie, J. *Narrative of the Siege of Londonderry*. London, 1890.

McNeill, R. *Ulster's Stand for Union*. London, 1922.

Mansergh, N. *The Government of Northern Ireland*. London, 1936.

Mansergh, P. *The Irish Question, 1840–1921*. London, 1965.

Maxwell, Constantia. *Irish History from Contemporary Sources, 1509–1610*. London, 1923.

Milligan, C. D. *The Walls of Derry*. 2 vols. Londonderry, 1948.

Milligan, C. D. *History of the Siege of Londonderry 1689*. Belfast, 1951.

Milton, John. *Complete Prose Works*. Vol. iii, ed. M. Y. Hughes. New Haven and London, 1962.

Moody, T. W. 'The Treatment of the Native Population Under the Scheme for the Plantation in Ulster'. In *Irish Historical Studies*, vol. i, no. 1 (1938).

Moody, T. W. *The Londonderry Plantation, 1609–41*. Belfast, 1939.

Moore, D., ed. *The Irish Sea Province in Archaeology and History*. Cardiff, 1970.

Moore, F. F. *The Truth About Ulster*. London, 1914.

Morton, G. 'The Enterprise of Ulster'. In *History Today*, vol. 17 (1967).

Morton, G. *Elizabethan Ireland*. London, 1971.

*Northern Whig*. 29 August 1857 and 18 June 1892.

O'Donnell, P. *The Irish Faction Fighters of the Nineteenth Century*. Dublin, 1975.

O'Rahilly, T. F. *Early Irish History and Mythology*. Dublin, 1971.

Percival-Maxwell, M. *The Scottish Migration to Ulster in the Reign of James I*. London, 1973.

Perrott, Sir John. *The Chronicle of Ireland*. Dublin, 1580.

Petrie, Sir Charles. 'The Jacobite War in Ireland, 1688–91', In *New English Review*, vol. xv, no. 1 (July 1947).

Phillips, Sir Thomas. *Londonderry and the London Companies, 1609–29*, ed. D. A. Chart. Belfast, 1928.

Quinn, D. B. *The Elizabethans and the Irish*. Ithaca, N.Y., 1966.

Reid, J. S. *History of the Presbyterian Church in Ireland*. 3 vols. Belfast, 1867.

*Reports from the Select Committee Appointed to Inquire into the Nature, Character, Extent and Tendency of Orange Lodges, Associations, or Societies in Ireland, with the Minutes of Evidence and Appendix*. First, second and third reports, 1835. (These and the following Reports were all published in London as Parliamentary Papers in the year after that in the title.)

*Report by the Commissioners of Inquiry into the Origins and Character of the Riots in Belfast in July and September 1857.*

*Report of the Commissioners of Inquiry, 1864, Respecting Magisterial and Police Jurisdiction, Arrangements and Establishment of the Borough of Belfast.*

*Report of the Commissioners of Inquiry, 1869, into the Riots and Disturbances in the City of Londonderry.*

*Report of a Commission Appointed to Inquire into Certain Disturbances Which Took Place in the City of Londonderry on 1 November 1883.*

*Report by the Commissioners of Inquiry, 1886, Respecting the Origins and Circumstances of the Riots in Belfast in June, July, August and September, 1886.*

Rodgers, R. J. 'The Rev. James Carlile' (unpublished Ph.D. thesis in the Queen's University, Belfast). 1973.

*Rutland MSS.* H.M.C., 14th Report, vol. iii. London, 1894.

Scott, Sir Walter. *Journal*, ed. W. E. K. Anderson. Oxford, 1972.

Senior, H. *Orangeism in Ireland and Britain, 1795–1836.* London, 1966.

Simms, J. G. *Jacobite Ireland 1685–91.* London, 1969.

*The Statutes at Large Passed in the Parliament held in Ireland.* 8 vols. Dublin, 1765.

Steele, E. D. *Irish Land and British Politics.*

Steele, E. D. 'Ireland for the Irish.' In *History*, June 1972.

Steiner, G. 'Ringing in the Old' (article in *The Listener*, 4 January 1973).

Stevenson, J. *Two Centuries of Life in Down 1600–1800.* Belfast, 1920.

Stewart, A. *History of the Church in Ireland . . . after the Scots were Naturalized*, ed. W. D. Killen, Belfast, 1866 (see Adair).

Sullivan, A. M. *New Ireland: Political Sketches and Personal Reminiscences.* 2 vols. London, 1878.

Tone, Theobald Wolfe. *Autobiography*, ed. R. Barry O'Brien, 2 vols. Dublin, 1893.

Trench, W. S. *Realities of Irish Life.* London, 1868 (reprint, London, 1966).

*Ulster Dialects: An Introductory Symposium.* Belfast, 1964.

Vincent, J. *The Origins of the Liberal Party.* London 1966.

Vogt, H. *Konfessionskrieg in Nordirland?* Stuttgart, 1973.

Walker, G. *A True Account of the Siege of Londonderry, 1689.* ed. P. Dwyer. London, 1893 (reprint, Belfast, 1971).

Wesley, John. *Journals, 1735–90*, ed. N. Curnock. 8 vols. London, 1909–16.

Whyte, J. H. *The Independent Irish Party, 1850–9.* Oxford, 1958.

Williams, T. Desmond, ed. *Secret Societies in Ireland.* London, 1973.

Witherow, T. *Derry and Enniskillen in the Year 1689.* Belfast, 1876.

Witherow, T. *Historical and Literary Memorials of Presbyterianism in Ireland.* 2 vols. Belfast, 1879.

Wright, T., ed. *Historical Works of Giraldus Cambrensis.* London, 1863.

Young, A. *Tour in Ireland.* 2 vols. ed. A. W. Hutton. London, 1892.

# Index